GOD IN OUR
PUBLIC SCHOOLS

GOD IN OUR PUBLIC SCHOOLS

By

W. S. FLEMING, D.D.

With Introduction by
LUTHER A. WEIGLE, Ph.D., D.D.
Dean of the Divinity School of Yale University

Published by
THE NATIONAL REFORM ASSOCIATION
209 NINTH STREET
PITTSBURGH, PENNSYLVANIA

Printed in the United States of America
By Light and Life Press
Winona Lake, Indiana

DEDICATED

TO THE MILLIONS OF AMERICAN CHILDREN, BORN AND YET TO BE, WHO NEVER, EXCEPT FROM THE SCHOOLTEACHER, WILL HEAR THE MESSAGE OF RELIGION AND MORALS THAT, ALONE, WILL ENABLE THEM TO BECOME GOOD CITIZENS.

PUBLISHER'S NOTE

The National Reform Association has undertaken the publication of this book because of its profound interest in restoring the Bible and instruction in nonsectarian religion to the public schools of America. Also because its Board of Directors believes the book with its masterly presentation of this subject will make a real and greatly needed contribution to the cause of Christian public education. For three-quarters of a century the Association by voice and pen has advocated the views so clearly and ably presented by Dr. Fleming in *God in Our Public Schools*. The co-operation of all who are interested in restoring the greatest character-building book in the world to its rightful place in our public schools is requested in securing for Dr. Fleming's book the widest possible reading.

The cost is $1.50 per copy, postpaid. It can be secured from The National Reform Association, 209 Ninth Street, Pittsburgh, Pennsylvania, and at many bookstores.

CONTENTS

INTRODUCTION

Beneath all other contributing factors, modern democracy is rooted in religious faith. Our ideals of freedom spring from faith in God. The sixteenth century brought the Bible to the people in their own tongue. "England," says Green in his *Short History of the English People,* "became the people of a book, and that book was the Bible. The whole temper of the nation felt the change. A new conception of life and of man superseded the old."

In the seventeenth century, this new conception of life challenged the absolutism of the Stuart kings. In the eighteenth century, the principles set forth in the Bill of Rights of 1689 were thought through and lived out on American soil, and they eventuated in our Declaration of Independence and the establishment of the United States of America.

"The basic postulate of the democratic faith," says Professor Ralph Gabriel in his objective study, *The Course of American Democratic Thought,* "affirmed that God, the

9

creator of man, has also created a moral law for his government and has endowed him with a conscience with which to apprehend it. Underneath and supporting human society, as the basic rock supports the hills, is a moral order which is the abiding place of the eternal principles of truth and righteousness."

From the point of view of the descriptive sciences, the first of the self-evident truths stated in our Declaration of Independence is not evident. It is simply not true that all men are created equal. But from the point of view of the law and love of God it is true, and that is the point of view that the authors of the Declaration took. They assumed the equality of men in the light of "the laws of nature and of nature's God." That means their equality before His impartial justice and His fatherly love. Faith in God underlies and is distinctly avowed in the Declaration of Independence. So only does the Declaration make sense.

The principle of the separation of church and state, as we hold it here in America, is often misunderstood and misapplied. It means just what the phrase implies—that church and state are mutually free. It means a separation of control so that neither church nor state will attempt to control the other. But it does not mean that the state acknowledges no God, or that the state is exempt from the moral law wherewith God sets the bounds of justice for nations as well as for individuals.

There is nothing in the status of the public school as an institution of the state, therefore, to render it godless. There is nothing in the principle of religious freedom or the separation of church and state to hinder the school's acknowledgement of the power and goodness of God. The common religious faith of the American people, as distinguished from the sectarian forms in which it is organized, may rightfully be assumed and find appropriate expression in the life and work of the public schools.

We must keep sectarianism out of our public schools. But that does not necessitate stripping the schools of religion. To exclude religion from the public schools would be to surrender these schools to the sectarianism of atheism or irreligion. To omit faith in God from our philosophy of education and from the program of our schools is to convey to children and youth a strong negative suggestion which tends to nullify rather than to fulfill our American principle of religious liberty. It is to undertake the impossible task of attempting to perpetuate and advance a culture—the American way of life—without informing our children as to the faith which has inspired and sustained that culture. It is to imperil the future of American democracy.

It is the merit of Dr. Fleming to have discerned these perils before many were awake to them, and to have devoted a considerable portion of his active life to service as a prophet and counselor with respect to the place in public education of faith in God. This book expresses the ripe experience of a man who has dealt with its subject throughout the length and breadth of the land. I honor his pioneering; I admire his devotion; and I have read his book with very great interest. It carries a message that America needs, and it puts that message in terms that all can understand.

LUTHER A. WEIGLE.

Yale University Divinity School.

FOREWORD

If religious public education means only another article of food in an already heavy diet for school children, this writer is not interested. If religious literacy means just a bit more knowledge, he does not care much. But when the words of such men as Horace Mann, Benjamin Kidd, Archbishop Ireland, Nicholas Murray Butler, Luther A. Weigle, Calvin Coolidge, John H. Finley, Charles Clayton Morrison, and other eminent thinkers urge that there is in public school religion some salt, some vitamin, a mysterious something that helps to immunize children against crime and secularism and tends to build them up into law-abiding religious citizens—then this author must investigate, and if facts seem to prove the theory, he must stand, heart and soul, for such education.

The first chapter of this book quotes the men. The fourth tests their theory. Whether you like statistics or not, facts alone provide the evidence that can prove or disprove a theory.

Official statistics show that within a few years after religion left the schools, crime began to grow and religion got into troubled waters, just as the men said they would, and both have grown worse to this moment; also, though as yet but little test can be made in reverse, when religion returned to some schools, conditions appeared to improve.

The statistics convinced the writer that the men quoted and many more that might have been quoted were not wishful thinkers, not false prophets, but discerning wise men, prophets of God. He therefore gives their words, backed by the evidence, that only God in our public schools can save this nation and our civilization from downfall through irreligion and crime. And that is the thesis of this book.

The book is no attack on any religious faith nor version of Scripture nor method of religious instruction. It is not a call to war, but points a way to peace and safety and right. The author believes that the way to meet a difficulty is not to dodge it, but to face it squarely, and he has tried to do that here with what he thinks good results.

The writer has all versions of Scripture

involved, and often uses them in public, not to show differences but resemblances. Instead of opposing any version in school, he says in Chapter VIII: "In mixed schools, why not several versions, including the Douay, on the teacher's desk for school use?"

There is no attack here on the Jew nor his religion. The author only digs up the law on the subject. This is a Christian nation, and the whole Bible has a right in our schools. The laws here give the Jew perfect religious liberty and a right to a happy home, but they do not put him on a pedestal above a Christian and give him a right to exclude the New Testament from our schools.

No unkind word is said about Catholics. Only such facts are told as seem relevant and helpful in solving the problem. Catholics are quoted several times with approval. It is even suggested that in large schools separate devotions might be desirable and should be granted.

In the closing chapter, Catholics, Protestants, and Jews are urged to co-operate and suggestions are made to that end.

Against parochial and released-time schools no word is said except that they cannot solve the problem we face. The book does say that when such schools are permitted, their proponents should be consistent and urge religion in public schools.

Homes and churches are not excused for any failure, nor is it sought to put upon the school any task of home or church. It is urged that all do all possible for the common good. It is emphasized that church and school have much in common and should co-operate for the good of all.

The problem is aggravated by the fact that we have not one educational system but forty-nine, one for each state and another for the Federal Government. The author does not advance his own thoughts but goes to wise men, to history, to statutes, to courts, to customs and lets these tell the story as far as possible.

Words about the author are of little importance. In 1910, the Illinois Supreme Court put the Bible out of the schools of that state. In 1918, the Chicago ministers' meeting of which he was and is a member, put upon him, against his protest, a three-months' intensive study of religious public education. In 1919, without his knowledge, his denominational head chose him to represent his denomination on a state commission of ten denominations to seek a provision in the proposed new state constitution plainly giving the Bible a right in the schools of the state. The commission made him executive secretary and sent him to the convention to lead the campaign. Friends in the body said, "You will disrupt the convention if you bring that religious issue here." Several months of intensive labor brought an all-day debate with no unkind word, and by a vote of fifty-three to nine, the convention gave the church people just what was asked. But Chicago and organized labor opposed certain provisions, and the new constitution died at the polls, the Bible sentence with the rest.

In that campaign, The National Reform Association gave laudable assistance. Finally leaders of that organization asked the writer to join their field force. On advice of his church superior, he accepted the offer as a call of duty, gave up a happy pastorate in Chicago, and for eleven years was a wanderer, speaking, writing, campaigning constantly in many states; and for ten years he declined to speak on any other subject than religious public education.

In the more than ten years since giving up the wandering life, he has continued the study of the subject. Now, he feels that he cannot pass from the scene of action without leaving in permanent form the facts and convictions that have come to him in the nearly twenty-five years' intensive study of the subject. Hence, *God in Our Public Schools.*

The author has no pecuniary interest in the publication of this book. With him it is purely a labor of love.

I cannot close this foreword without acknowledging my debt to the many persons who have given much and valued help in the preparation of this book. Grateful thanks are expressed to Dr. Luther A. Weigle, dean of the Divinity School of Yale University, for writing the introduction and also for helpful suggestions; also to the following for reading the manuscript and making valued criticisms and suggestions: Dr. Ward W. Keesecker, United States Office of Education, Washington, D. C., whose contribution was personal rather than official; Professor S. A. Graves, dean of the College of Liberal Arts, Detroit Institute of Technology; Dr. H. L. Cleland, director of Personnel,

Pittsburgh Public Schools; Rev. E. J. Vandervort; and Mr. E. Clay Young, secretary of the Pennsylvania Gideons. My thanks, also, to M. Gyla MacDowell, Litt.D., of Geneva College, for assistance in putting the manuscript in form for publication, and to Miss Marian F. Wiegel for typing it.

My thanks, also, to Rev. J. S. Martin, D.D. and his brother, Rev. R. H. Martin, D.D., my chiefs of former days, for their criticisms and laborious services in preparing the manuscript for publication. These and many others have my grateful thanks.

W. S. F.

July 1, 1942

I

THE SCHOOLS MAKE THE NATION

Do not the schools make the nation? Is not this what they are for? Why else a permanent capital investment of over six billion dollars? Why else an annual operating expense of two and a half billion dollars? Why else a school-house and a state-paid teacher within the reach of every child under the flag? Why else must every child in the land be in school six hours a day, five days a week, nine or ten months a year for ten to twelve years, the most impressionable years of life? Why else do we choose a million of the most intelligent, conscientious, faithful, best-trained men and women in the nation and pay them to educate our children? Why else is public education free and compulsory? Why else does the state force its hand into your pocket and mine and take from us the money it needs to run the schools? Why else, if I am a pauper and you a millionaire, does the state compel you to educate my child? Why all this and much more if the schools do not make the nation?

The fathers were wise. They knew that if democracy is to survive and prosper, every citizen must have a keen brain and a clean life. They knew that many parents could not or would not educate their children. They knew that the churches could not educate all the children, for no power on earth can compel a parent to send his child to church. They also knew that to leave the task to the churches, as many now insist, would be a union of church and state, with the state not a sovereign but a weakling, drinking its very lifeblood from an institution it could not control. So the state buckled down to the job and built the schools, the most outreaching and finest institution under the flag. The state planned the type of curriculum needed to make the kind of citizens it must have. And the state compels every child to go to school whether parents like it or not, thereby assuming the role of super-parent. Of course the aim of the state in all this is self-preservation, the highest good of all. But do the schools make the nation? Some expert testimony follows:

Benjamin Kidd said:

"The idealism of mind and spirit conveyed to the young of each generation under the influence of the social passion, is absolutely limitless in its effects. The power which is represented thereby is capable of creating a new world in the life-time of a generation. It is capable of sweeping away in a single generation any existing order of the world."[1]

Mr. Kidd shows that Germany was transformed in a single generation from a peace-loving people to the most warlike nation the modern world has seen. He says that when the Kaiser came to the throne (in 1888) he called the primary and elementary teachers of his realm together and made a speech deifying himself and glorifying war. He ordered all teachers from kindergarten to university to teach his principles in the schools of Germany. And they did. Soon the schools of the nation rang with deification of the Kaiser and the glorification of war. Thus in twenty-six years the World War burst upon humanity. Kidd says it was exactly the same teaching in the schools that "created that other utterly unforeseen and incalculable phenomenon of the modern world, the new-born power of Japan." He also holds that only in this same way can "universal peace" be brought about. Were Mr. Kidd writing in these second World War days he would doubtless note that the present blood-and-iron education in German schools for world conquest is really "education for death" not only to Germany but to the whole human race.

Mr. Kidd's dictum, in short, is just this— *what you put into the schools will in from twenty to thirty years be a controlling force in the lives of the people. Or conversely.*

We in America have proved this dictum. About 1890 every state passed compulsory scientific temperance instruction laws for all our schools. Soon every schoolhouse rang with the evil effects of intoxicants. What was the result? In twenty-nine years we wrote the Eighteenth Amendment into the Constitution. Then we held a great celebration over the grave of John Barleycorn and quietly dropped temperance instruction from our schools and Sunday schools and in less than fifteen years the Twenty-first Amendment killed the Eighteenth.

Archbishop Ireland, one of the great leaders of the Roman Catholic Church half a century ago, made a most remarkable address before the National Educational Association in Saint Paul, Minnesota, in 1890. In this speech he said:

"In our fear lest Protestants gain some advantage over Catholics or Catholics over Protestants, we play into the hands of unbelievers and secularists. We have given over to them the schools, the nursery of thought. Are we not securing for them the mastery of the future? The state school is nonreligious. It teaches of land and sea but not of God and Christ; it tells how to attain success in this world, but says nothing of the world beyond the grave. The pupil sees and listens, and insensibly forms the conclusion that religon is of minor importance. Religious indifference becomes his creed. . . . The very life of our civilization and of our country is at stake. The American school as it first reared its log walls in the villages of New England was religious through and through. The favor with which the nonreligious state school is regarded is, I verily believe, due to the thoughtlessness of the moment and will not last. I would permeate the regular state school with the religion of the majority, be that religion as Protestant as Protestantism can be."[2]

Prof. C. F. Paulus, in a book every young

Methodist minister was required to study forty years ago, said:

> "The injurious effects of the want of religion in our schools is already to be seen in the frequent complaints about the increasing impiety of 'young Americans,' and about the increasing number of juvenile criminals. But the worst is yet to be unless this wound of our public education is healed. Whenever religion is ignored in the public schools, the Christian disposition must vanish and make way for sin and vice."[3]

James Russell Lowell said:

> "The problem before us is to make a whole of our many discordant parts, our many foreign elements, and I know of no way in which this can better be done than by providing a common system of education."[4]

Nicholas Murray Butler, President of Columbia University, in his annual report of 1934, said:

> "The separation of church and state is fundamental in our American political order, but so far as religious instruction is concerned, this principle has been so far departed from as to put the whole force and influence of the tax-supported schools on the side of one element of the population, namely, that which is pagan and believes in no religion whatever."[5]

Luther A. Weigle, Dean of the Yale University Divinity School, has been saying over the land for many years:

> "The secularization of public education in America has issued in a situation fraught with danger. The situation is such as to imperil, in time, the future of religion among the people, and, with religion the future of the nation itself. A system of public education that gives no place to religion is not in reality neutral, but exerts an influence, unintentional though it be, *against* religion. For the state not to include in its educational program a definite recognition of the place and value of religion in human life is to convey to children, with all the prestige and authority of the school maintained by the state, the suggestion that religion has no real place and value. The omission of religion from the public schools of today conveys a condemnatory suggestion to the children."[6]

Horace Mann is the father of our American public school system. He was a lawyer and for some years a member of the Massachusetts Legislature. In 1837, he became secretary of the Massachusetts State Board of Education. This position he held for twelve years. He then went to Congress to succeed John Quincy

Adams. He brought every power of his mind to
bear upon the public school system, then feeble
and struggling for its existence. He founded
and edited the *Common School Journal,*
held teachers' institutes, established normal
schools, lectured widely on educational subjects
and, best of all, wrote twelve annual reports,
each one a good-sized volume. Very few subjects have come before educational leaders today that were not frankly and fully discussed
in his reports. Their depth and insight and
breadth of view is marvelous, and their influence in spreading and fixing the Massachusetts
school system over and upon the nation is
beyond comprehension. Our interest in his
reports has to do with religion and morals. It
is often suggested that he opposed religion in
the schools and tried to exclude it therefrom,
but the exact opposite is the truth. He opposed
sectarian books that certain financial interests
sought to get into school libraries and incurred
the bitter enmity of those interests, but won in
the battle.[7] He found the Bible being gradually dropped from the schools and labored ear-
nestly and succeeded well in getting it restored.
Horace Mann was one of the most earnest advo-

cates of religion in the schools that the nation has produced. Three of his twelve annual reports give large space to the subject of religion: those of 1843, 1847, and 1848, with occasional favorable comments on the same topic in others. In the report of 1847 he said:

"The use of the Bible in the schools is not expressly enjoined by law, but both its letter and its spirit are consonant with that use, and, as a matter of fact, I suppose there is not, at the present time, a single town in the commonwealth in whose schools it is not read."[8]

In his final report, Mr. Mann devoted thirty-five pages to moral and religious instruction in the schools. He says:

"Moral education is a primal necessity of social existence. The grand result in practical morals ... can never be attained without religion, and no community will ever be religious without a religious education ... Had the Board required me to exclude either the Bible or religious instruction from the schools, I certainly should have given them the earliest opportunity to appoint my successor."[9]

In these days when the nation rocks and reels with crime, when men insist that the fault lies in home and church and that the schools have nothing to do with religion, it may call us back

to sanity to see what Mr. Mann did in the matter
and to learn his conclusions. In his 1847 report,
he considered the subject at great length. He
prepared a long circular letter, and set forth
the conditions of vice and crime. He noted the
possibilities of moral and religious instruction
in the public schools with proper teachers,
under laws substantially the same then as now.
He suggested that all external conditions—the
home and the church, etc., remain the same.
He conditioned that all children from four to
sixteen years of age be in public schools ten
months each year. He then asked what proportion of the children would become respectable
members of society. He sent the letter to nine
prominent teachers in five states, asking them
to answer in the light of their own experience.
All replied. He quotes all the letters. Every
one says that 99 per cent to 100 per cent of the
children would become good citizens. He then
shows that many schools fully measure up to
the conditions and that all, with no change of
law either as to curriculum or character of the
teachers, might do so. Then he moralizes
through many pages, especially on the financial
advantages of the proper education of children.

The cost of a common drunk in court on Monday morning would educate two children for a year. The keep of one major criminal would educate a hundred children.

On the closing page of his final report, he envisaged the public schools as the instrument of "replenishing the common mind with knowledge, and the common heart with virtue." He saw the great uninhabited West, now the central states, as the future "empire reclaimed to a Christian life and a Christian history," or a center of "profligacy, licentiousness and corrupt civilization," and he begged his native state "to send out the influence of her schools to save the vast West from such a perdition."[10]

It should be added that the laws against sectarianism in the schools passed by the states generally in the '70's were adopted in Massachusetts in 1827, ten years before Mr. Mann began his work, so that the laws under which he labored were practically the same as the laws over the nation today.

John D. Pierce was chosen state superintendent of the schools of Michigan in 1836 when that state applied to come into the Union. He was born in New England. Immediately after his appointment he went to Massachusetts and spent six months studying the school system of that state, and upon his return set up the schools of the new state after the Massachusetts model. His biographers say: "In his day schools were distinctly religious in character, and it was not necessary to say anything in favor of religious teaching in them."[11] In his third annual report to the legislature he said:

"Our safety is not in constitutions and forms of government, but in the establishment of a right system of education. Every child in the state shall be educated and fitted to fulfill his duty faithfully to his country and his God."[12]

In his fifth and final report in 1841, he said:

"We must provide all the necessary means of instruction for the whole population, or greatly increase the number of jails, penitentiaries and standing armies. We must educate or forge bolts, bars and chains."[13]

John H. Finley, recently deceased, formerly Commissioner of Education of New York State and President of the University of the State of New York, quotes with approval words written by Dr. Henry L. Smith of Washington-Lee University, as follows:

"Let but one generation of American boys and girls be rightly trained in body, mind and spirit, in knowledge and love and unselfishness, and all the knotty problems of our American life, social, economic and political would be far on the road toward complete solution. Let the training of but one generation be wholly neglected and our civilization, losing its art, science, literature and religion would be far on the road to primeval savagery. The right training of the young is the spiritual reproduction of the race, the flower of the nation's civilization, the supreme test and the most accurate of its wisdom and culture."[14]

Calvin Coolidge, when Vice-President in April, 1923, gave a public address in which he said in part:

"The secular theory of the state cannot stand. Unless destroyed it will shake this nation to its foundations; no nation ever has stood without religion. No nation ever will stand without religion. No nation ever can stand without religion. If a sparrow cannot fall to the ground without the notice of God, a nation cannot stand without His aid. And He cannot aid a nation that ignores Him. The forms and power of religion must permeate the state and be recognized by it. The public school is the one place to put religion to make it effective in national life."[15]

Charles Clayton Morrison, Editor of *The Christian Century,* said, in public address to the 10,000 teachers of Missouri in Kansas City, November 9, 1940:

> "The public school is confessedly and deliberately secular. I am bound therefore to lay on the doorstep of our educational system the prime responsibility for the decline of religion and the steady advance of secularism, another term for atheism, in American society."[16]

The verdict. From a great multitude that might be called, we have eleven men, all high-grade, discerning thinkers, covering a period of over 100 years, who agree that *the schools make the nation,* and some insist that *the present secularized public school is destroying religion and wrecking the nation through crime.*

THE SCHOOLS MAKE THE NATION

REFERENCES

1. Kidd, Benjamin, *Science of Power.* G. J. Putnam and Sons, New York. pages 125-154; pages 308, 309.
2. Ireland, John, Address, *Proceedings National Educational Association,* St. Paul, Minnesota, 1890. Pages 179-184.
3. Paulus, Charles F., *The Christian Life.* Cranston and Stowe, 1892. Pages 381-384.
4. Lowell, James Russell, *Democracy and other Addresses.* Houghton, Mifflin Co., 1887. Page 132.
5. Butler, Nicholas Murray, *Bulletin of Information,* Columbia University, 1934. Page 22.
6. Weigle, Luther A., *Federal Council Bulletin,* November-December, 1923. Page 20.
7. Culver, Raymond B., *Horace Mann and Religion in Massachusetts Public Schools.* Yale University Press, 1929. Chaps. V, VI, VIII, IX.
8. Mann, Horace, *Annual Reports.* H. B. Fuller, 1868. Page 595.
9. Ibid., pages 701-717.
10. Ibid., page 757.
11. Hoyt and Ford, *Life of John D. Pierce.* Page 100.
12. Ibid., page 94.
13. Ibid., page 94.
14. Finley, John H., *The Debt Eternal,* by Missionary Board. Page 181.
15. *The Ministers Monthly,* September, 1923.
16. *The Christian Century.* May 7, 1941.

II

EARLY PUBLIC SCHOOLS RELIGIOUS

Early American schools were permeated with religion. The only question is whether they were church schools or state schools. In 1635, a town meeting in Massachusetts Bay Colony appointed a schoolmaster.[1] In 1642, a law was passed holding to the grand jury any man who failed to see that his child was able "to read and understand the principles of religion and the capital laws of the country."[2] In 1645, Dorchester made the "first public provision in the world for a free school supported by direct taxation on the inhabitants of the town."[3] In 1647, the Massachusetts School Ordinance was passed providing for schools in townships having fifty families.[4] The words "town meeting," "grand jury," "inhabitants," "township" in all these indicated that the action was taken by the people in a civil rather than in an ecclesiastical capacity; hence they were public and not church schools. More-

over, religion was the dominant note in all.
Led by the Bay State such were the schools of
New England all through the colonial period.
"When I was young the books used were chiefly
or wholly Dilworth's Spelling Books, the Psal-
ter, the Testament and the Bible,"[5] writes Noah
Webster, speaking of his childhood schools in
Connecticut, where he was born in 1758.

The New England Primer was the book
mainly used in those early schools. It passed
through many editions. Copies of it are available today in public libraries, and these show
that the book was distinctly religious. A picture and a single line introduce each letter of
the alphabet, and usually both picture and line
are religious. The little bedtime prayer, "Now
I lay me down to sleep," is there. There we
find the nursery hymn, "Hush, my dear, lie
still and slumber." Bible names, verses, and
facts make up a good part of the text. "Pray
to God," "Love God," "Serve God," "Fear
God"—these are among its lessons. A. A.
Brown says, *"The New England Primer* was
essentially a child's book of religion. It and
the Bible maintained their supremacy (in the
schools) through the colonial period."[6]

Outside of New England, various types of schools appeared. New York City and State vied with New England in the use of public education. Parish schools were very common with poor children educated at public expense. *But whatever the type of school, religion was the dominant chord.*

The Public School

Public education developed slowly after the Revolution. Early in the new century, the New England and New York schools won the day and became the type of school over the nation, with the Bible and its message always a vital part of instruction. In July, 1941, I spent five hours in the Rochester, New York, Public Library examining forty different books used about a century ago in the schools of that section—readers, grammars, spellers. There were many different authors and publishers of these books, dated from 1811 to 1840, with one or two a little later. *Murray's Grammar* was in its twenty-eighth edition in 1821. Two facts very relevant here stood out clearly: 1. Instead of public schools being of recent birth, they were of long standing and widely popular all over the northeastern part of the country a century ago; 2. Religion was then universal in the schools, for every one of those old books was full of religion and morals.

In 1829, the public school system of Cincinnati was set up with the Bible in the schools.[7] As already seen, Michigan began her school system in 1836 with religion as an essential element. In 1844, New York State passed a law forbidding exclusion of the Bible from the schools of New York City on sectarian grounds. That law now stands and is obeyed. In 1855, Massachusetts said by law that the Bible must be used daily in all schools, and that law is obeyed today. In 1858, Iowa passed a law forbidding exclusion of the Bible from her schools. Indiana followed in 1865, West Virginia in 1866, Florida in 1869, Mississippi in 1870. In 1870, Mr. Cameron said in the Illinois State Constitutional Convention: "Custom has generally established the Bible in our public schools."[8] Evidently the public school is older than some would have us think. It followed the mover's wagon out of New England and New York, and wherever the school went, the Bible went, essential in public education.

An old copy of *McGuffey's Fifth Reader,* the book used all over the nation for half a century before 1890, lies on my desk as I write. Of the two hundred and thirty-five lessons of this book, sixty-three have a religious flavor, and many more a moral value. Webster's blue-backed spelling book, used very widely for fifty years before 1875 and with over sixty million copies printed, was full of religion and morals.

The common schools of those days had a high religious and moral tone and turned out men and women who lived right and made the nation great, and made it as good as it was great.

Early Higher Education Religious

Religion was also prominent in higher education in those days. The school of higher learning that shies at nothing but religion is a modern innovation.

University of Virginia—No man in American history has been more misrepresented and maligned in matters religious than Thomas Jefferson. In 1776, a generation too early for the rest, he suggested a comprehensive system of state schools. He repeated the suggestion in

1814. As to religion in common schools, his attitude does not appear. For secondary schools he wanted ethics with a religious base. In "Professional Schools" he would have "Theological and Ecclesiastical History," not unlike present theological seminaries. At his suggestion, in 1818, the Virginia Legislature appointed a committee, of which he was made chairman, to set up a state university and prepare a curriculum. He wrote the report and suggested a program, and the legislature adopted it all and made him head of the committee to set up the university.[9] The whole project will be considered later. Here it can only be said that religion was a prominent element in the program.

The University of Michigan began in 1837, and one of the first rules required students to attend chapel daily and to go to church once a week. This rule stood for fifty years.[10] President O. E. Haven, later a Methodist Bishop, held that the university must be nonsectarian but decidedly religious. A normal course was put in, and all prospective teachers were required to study McIlvaine's *Evidences of Christianity,* one of the greatest theological works of the nineteenth century, thoroughly nonsectarian but deeply religious.

A suggestive incident happened in 1851-2. One of the professors, D. D. Whedon, who later became one of the greatest Methodist theologians of the century, was dismissed because he advocated, as stated in the resolution of dismissal, a "doctrine which is unauthorized by the Bible and at war with the principles of Christ and His apostles." The resolution was presented and the battle led by Abner Pratt, then a member of the Supreme Court of the state, who evidently thought the university a watchdog of orthodoxy.[11]

The University of Illinois opened its doors in 1868. For many years all students were required to attend chapel daily, and the State Supreme Court sustained the school in enforcing the rule against a plea of religious liberty raised by a student.

In the light of all the above how does it come about that religion and education are so completely divorced today?

EARLY PUBLIC SCHOOLS RELIGIOUS

REFERENCES

1. Brown, Arlo A., *A History of Religious Education in Modern Times*. Published by Abingdon Press, page 33.
2. Ibid., page 34.
3. Goucher, John F., *Christianity and the United States*. Published by Eaton and Mains, page 28.
4. Brown *op. Cit.* 34.
5. Cubberley, Elwood P., *History of Education*, page 369.
6. Brown, *op. Cit.*, page 39.
7. *Ohio Supreme Court Reports*, 23 Ohio 211.
8. *Proceedings, Illinois Constitutional Convention*, 1870. page 1744.
9. Cabell, Joseph C., *History of University of Virginia and Letters of Jefferson and Cabell*. Published by J. W. Randolph, 1856, pages 441 and 474.
10. *Minutes of Regents University of Michigan*, Nov. 3, 1857.
11. Ibid., Dec. 31, 1851.

III

PUBLIC EDUCATION SECULARIZED

General statement. Very generally religion left the schools in the '70's, and today it seems to be in much of the nation the one subject against which schoolhouse doors are bolted and barred. How the change was made is not well understood. It is not easy to explain. But the facts should be known. *The Book did not leave the schools by the will of the people.* Three far-western states—Washington, Utah, and Arizona—according to an apparently correct ruling of the Supreme Court of Washington, have constitutional bars, all alike, against the Book in tax-supported schools. East of the Rockies, no such law can be found. None exists. Nor was the Book dropped through legal opinions or administrative rulings except perhaps in New York State. Such legal opinions as now exist were made after the Book was gone, not before, and seem results, not causes, of the change. How then did the Book go? It was in the schools by custom not by mandatory law. Alien minorities, one or two in a community, went quietly to the teacher and demanded that the Bible be dropped, and the teachers, being teachers not warriors, reluctantly obeyed. The deed was done while the majority were asleep. The Book that made our civilization left the schools as quietly as night follows day. *The Bible was not legislated out of the schools; it was quietly crowded out by alien influence and indifference.*

New York City and State. Opposition to the Bible in the school seems to have reached public officials first in New York State about 1837. For over a hundred years the ruling in that state has been that, if opposition appears, there shall be no Bible reading during school hours. Its reading is thus prohibited on prudential instead of legal grounds. And that ruling has largely closed the doors of upstate schools against the Bible.

In the City, the question took a different turn. Public schools and sectarian schools sprang up side by side. Soon some Protestants asked tax money for their schools, and got the money. Public sentiment gradually turned against tax money for church schools, and the money was at last refused. Protestants were the first to ask and the first to be denied. This denial was in 1824. In 1840, Roman Catholics asked for tax money and were refused. In 1842, the legislature passed a law applying to the city only, forbidding tax money to any school in which "any religious sectarian doctrine or tenet shall be taught, inculcated, or practiced." Catholics must have interpreted this, as excluding the King James Bible from the schools, for in 1844, the legislature added to the law, "Nothing herein contained shall authorize the Board of Education to exclude the Holy Scriptures, without note or comment, or any selection therefrom, from any of the schools provided for in this act." In 1898, the words of the above statute were put into the special charter given New York City, and they are there today. The same year, the city school board adopted a rule, probably reaffirming an old rule, requiring the daily reading of the Bible in all city schools, and that rule still stands. Thus apparently the Bible has been used in the schools of the nation's metropolis during all the history of these schools from about 1800.

Note. Plainly the restriction in the law of 1844 "without note or comment" did not tell teachers *how* to use the Bible but, *what* Bible to use, that is, one with no notes or comments.

Massachusetts. In 1827, the state forbade using public funds for sectarian purposes, not to get sectarianism out of the schools, but to keep it out, for it was then nearly gone, as Mr. Mann said. As seen above, Horace Mann restored the Bible to the schools. But after he quit the school system, the Book must again have begun to disappear, for in 1855, the legislature passed a law requiring the daily reading of the Bible in all schools, and that law still stands and is obeyed. In 1859, opponents sought in court, without avail, to shut the Scriptures out of the schools of Boston. In 1866, the State Supreme Court held the Bible in the schools against the plea of objectors. Hence the Bible never left the schools of the Bay State. It is used there today in all schools.

Conflict over the nation. In 1854, the Supreme Court of Maine, the first high court in the nation to face the question, rejected the plea of a Catholic father to throw the Bible out of the schools of that state. Up to 1870, opponents of the Book of God in the schools had fought battles before two State Supreme Courts—Massachusetts and Maine—and seven State legislatures—New York, Massachusetts, Iowa, Indiana, West Virginia, Florida and Mississippi—and lost every battle. But on November 1, 1869, a battle was joined that brought swift and almost complete victory to the enemies of the Bible in the schools.

The Cincinnati case. By school board rule, the Bible had been in daily use in all schools since they were organized in 1829. Several times, Catholics had asked for tax money for their schools, but the requests had always been denied. They complained that certain books in the schools were unfair to them, but never specified which books. Finally, on November 1, 1869, without warning and with no recent complaint that we can find, by vote of 24 to 14, the school board forbade all religious exercises in the schools, putting the Bible under ban by name, the only instance we can find where the Book was named. Many people were shocked. Many believed that the Book had fundamental right in the schools and that the school board could not exclude it. The case went to the state supreme court, and in 1872, that body held that the school board rules the school and may, if it wishes, exclude the Bible. The court did not hold that the Bible has no right in the schools. It did say that under Ohio law, the school board rules the school, and may, if it wishes, exclude the Bible. The court even suggested that the legislature might be asked to change the law on the subject. But no appeal was made to the legislature, and the Bible remained out of the schools of Cincinnati.

The case aroused nation-wide interest. Much was said by counsel on both sides not germane to the subject. Much was said by the court that did not touch the main issue, *obiter dicta,* as the lawyers say. What was said against religion in the schools was eagerly taken up by the opposition and broadcasted over the nation. The public was given a wrong impression. It was led to believe that religion has no right in the public schools.

Sectarian use of tax money. This question had been agitated since about 1820. Protestants gave up private education and patronized public schools, but Catholics set up parochial schools wherever possible and persistently asked for public funds. The matter was much alive in the '70's. Following the 1827 law in Massachusetts and that of 1842 in New York, many states passed laws forbidding giving tax money to sectarian schools. At the suggestion of President Grant in his annual message to Congress, December 14, 1875, James G. Blaine introduced into the lower house a proposed amendment to the Federal Constitution forbidding states to give public money for sectarian purposes, and the proposal passed the House of Representatives by a vote of 180 to 7. By a vote of 27 to 15, the Senate added to the proposal the words, "This article shall not be construed to prohibit the reading of the Bible in any public school or institution," and then, by a vote of 28 to 16, killed the whole proposal. Catholics were very anxious for tax money for their schools, and their opposition killed the measure.

The two questions tied together. We believe that for years Catholics had tied the two questions together, just as the Senate did, though Protestants saw no connection between the two. We find no instance of Catholic opposition to the Bible in the schools until they were refused public money for their schools. Then they, playing politics, seemed to say, "No money for our schools, no Bible for your schools." Many years ago a Chicago Catholic judge, Timothy D. Hurley, now deceased, told me as much.

The result. Catholics continued their fight against the Bible in the schools, still hoping to get tax money. The states were opposed to their having it and passed laws, as above stated, forbidding such appropriations. As hinted by the above vote of the United States Senate on the subject, the laws and court decisions of many states plainly show that these laws were not to exclude the Bible from the schools, but to tell sectarian groups that they could not have tax money for their schools. Samuel Wisner Brown is wrong when in his *Secularization of American Education* he says, "Secularization came about ... by the passage of laws excluding religion from the schools." Catholics went neither to courts nor legislatures, for there they had met too many defeats. No law was passed shutting the Book from the schools. No case went to the courts in those days. Individuals went quietly to school teachers and demanded that the Book be dropped. Probably some help came from Jews and Missouri Synod Lutherans, each for reasons of their own. It was a gumshoe battle, all standing for what they thought right. There was no squabble, as some charge, among the churches. Dr. Weigle is right, that the result was "incidental not intentional," at least among Protestants. People generally did not know what was going on, and even the instigators did not realize the fearful consequences to flow from it. But the Book left the schoolhouses as leaves fall in autumn, and school doors were shut in the face of God. Nor can Catholics be blamed overmuch for they were evidently sincere. Nevertheless schools were secularized. God was excluded, and the nation's downfall began.

PUBLIC EDUCATION SECULARIZED

PRINCIPAL AUTHORITIES CONSULTED FOR THIS CHAPTER

Hall. Arthur J., *Religious Education in the Public Schools of the State and City of New York.* University of Chicago Press.

Brown, Samuel W., *Secularization of American Education.* Teachers College, Columbia University, 1912.

Minor, John D. et al., *The Bible in the Public Schools.* Robert Clarke and Company, 1872.

The Bible in the Public Schools, Superior Court of Cincinnati, 1872 .

Congressional Record. First Session, 44th Congress. *House Proceedings,* page 205. Also pages 5189-5192. *Senate Proceedings,* pages 5580-5595.

IV

THE NATION TODAY

All believers in God hold that when religion declines, crime grows, and that when religion flourishes, crime decreases. Only atheists, like Maurice Parmelee, the government-dismissed employee of recent nudist fame, deny this, and thus show their folly.

The present question. What, if anything, happened to the American way of life in morals and religion when religion left the schools? The first chapter shows that the specific task of the schools is to build our defensive bulwarks and the road of progress, particularly in matters of intelligence and character. In that chapter eleven prominent men, covering a period of a century, were quoted by name who held in substance that the schools make the nation. Three of them, Benjamin Kidd, John H. Finley, and Henry L. Smith, said that an ideal put into the schools would in a generation dominate the nation, and what leaves the schools will soon leave the nation. Two earlier men, Horace Mann and John D. Pierce, urged that if religious instruction leaves the schools, religion will suffer and crime flourish. Different ones of the later men—Archbishop Ireland, Charles F. Paulus, Nicholas Murray Butler, Calvin Coolidge, Luther A. Weigle, Charles Clayton Morrison—after the schools became secular and as a result of that act, saw religion suffering and crime growing; "pagan" control of the schools; religion becoming of "minor importance" in the public mind; "religious indifference" becoming our "creed"; schools "not neutral but in effect against religion"; "the decline of religion and the steady advance of secularism, another name for atheism." Different ones held that secular education, if continued, will produce a situation "fraught with danger"; "will shake the nation to its foundations"; will "imperil the future of the nation"; will endanger "the life of our civilization"; will "destroy the inner citadel of democracy, the last defense of civilization"; and bring upon us "profligacy, licentiousness and corrupt civilization."

Those words made by men whose standing should give every American instant and serious pause, are a terrible indictment. The charge is not against the schools as such. They are the finest institution under the flag, the just pride of every American. The indictment is not against the teachers, who are as earnest, able, devoted, loyal, and religious as any group in the nation. It is against us, the people, who permitted God to be expelled from the schools.

Is the indictment sustained by the evidence? Are the men who bring the charge wise, far-seeing statesmen, prophets of God? Or are they false prophets?

The indictment further sustained. Theodore Roosevelt said, "A man trained in mind but not in morals is a menace to society." Calvin Coolidge declares, "Education without character is dangerous." Nicholas Murray Butler affirms, "Our schools turn out intellectual giants and moral pygmies." Roger Babson writes, "Trying to operate the schools without religion is like putting a pistol into the hands of a child." Sam Jones says, "You can't teach old dogs new tricks, but you can help the pups."

An old adage runs, "As the twig is bent the tree is inclined." George Washington insists, "Reason and experience forbid us to expect that national morality can prevail in the exclusion of religious principles." The Bible says, "Train up a child in the way he should go, and when he is old he will not depart from it."

But all the above are assertions, expert testimony perhaps, and yet only opinion, theory. What about experience? Has crime increased, has religion suffered since God was shut out of the schools? Whether we like statistics or not, only these can prove whether the men quoted in the first chapter were false prophets or farsighted statesmen.

The Growth of Crime

On April 29, 1929, soon after his inauguration President Hoover addressed representatives of the Associated Press on what he called "the dominant issue before the American people." He said: "Its solution is more vital to the preservation of our institutions than any other question before us. With us life and property are relatively more unsafe than in any other civilized nation. We have twenty times as many murders and fifty times as many robberies in proportion to population as Great Britain. We suffer not from an ephemeral crime wave but from a subsidence of our foundations." He appointed a commission of eleven men, the Wickersham Commission, to study the crime situation and suggest a remedy. The plan failed because he put ten lawyers and but one teacher on the commission.

Marcus A. Kavanaugh, for over thirty years an honored Chicago judge, said in the April, 1925, *Journal of the American Bar Association:*

> "We have at large and unpunished in the United States at least 135,000 crimson-handed women and men who unlawfully have taken human life. They exceed in number all clergymen of all denominations. They are more numerous than all our male teachers put together. There was never another situation like this in the civilized world."

About 1923, the national convention of the American Bar Association adopted the report of a special committee appointed the year before to study the crime situation. The report said:

> "In major crimes this country is now the most lawless civilized nation on the globe, and the condition has been growing worse since 1890."

NUMBER OF PERSONS ARRESTED AGES 16 TO 24

Data Compiled From Fingerprint Cards • January 1 To December 31, 1941

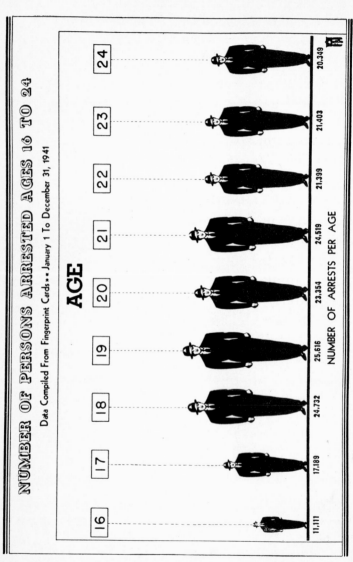

AGE

16	17	18	19	20	21	22	23	24
11,111	17,189	24,732	25,616	23,354	24,519	21,399	21,403	20,349

NUMBER OF ARRESTS PER AGE

Federal Bureau of Investigation—John Edgar Hoover, Director

Government prison reports sound the alarm.
In 1904, we had in prison 69 convicts for every
100,000 of our population. The number was
75 in 1910. It was 85 in 1927. It was 100 in
1934, and on January 1, 1939, it was 124, an
increase of 80 per cent in 34 years. And the
increase came not from new laws but from the
same old laws against murder, robbery, and
rape.

One of the most disheartening phases of the
sad situation is the relative increase of youth-
ful criminals. A very recent graph from J.
Edgar Hoover shows that youth of 19 furnish
more criminals than any other age.

On March 6, 1942, Chief Justice Dunn, of
the Chicago Criminal Court, said in public
address:

> "Half the defendants coming into our criminal
> courts are teen-age youths. What is happening to
> America? It is disheartening to the judges to see
> this vast number of youth between 15 and 21
> coming here daily."

An up-to-the-minute report on crime came
from Mr. J. Edgar Hoover on March 24, 1942,
when from New York City on the Knights of
Columbus radio broadcast, he said:

"Even today, each time your watch ticks off a minute, three serious crimes are committed. Every seven and one-half minutes a murder or serious assault occurs in our nation. All because too often moral responsibility has been unknown to those who commit the crimes."

Beyond question, we are going down hill faster and faster, and youth leads us to destruction.

Victor Hugo said, "When you open a school you close a prison." But we Americans have not found it so. We have a public school for every child under the flag, and all children must go to school. But we cannot build prisons fast enough, and every prison is crowded. In 1904, one person in every 1,540 of the nation was in prison. On January 1, 1939, one in every 825 was behind prison bars, and prison commitments increased 4.7 per cent during 1938. Something is terribly wrong.

Perhaps the most disheartening part of it all is that we do not seem to be much surprised, not at all shocked by the facts. For half a century, since 1890, as the lawyers reported above, the moral fibre of the nation has been loosening. Deep-seated causes have been at work, seen by few, but tremendously operative. This moral breakdown, this holocaust of crime is not a functional disorder, like measles, a mere temporary discomfort. It is an organic malady, a consumption, gnawing at the vitals of the nation, and it will destroy us in time unless we find and remove the cause.

The Struggle of Religion

In his farewell address, parts of which sound almost as though they came direct from heaven, Washington said:

> "Of all the dispositions and habits which lead to political prosperity, religion and morality are indispensable supports. . . . Where is the security for property, for reputation, for life, if the sense of religious obligation deserts the oaths which are the instruments of investigation in courts of justice? Let us indulge with caution the supposition that morality can be maintained without religion. . . . Reason and experience forbid us to expect that national morality can prevail in the exclusion of religious principles."

Back of the words of Washington and multitudes who speak like him is the universal verdict of history that "Righteousness exalteth a nation, but sin is a reproach to any people."

A religious citizenship is doubly necessary in a democracy where every citizen is a king in his own right, in a nation where every adult has the ballot and may hold public office, and especially in a nation where every child must go to school and sharpen his wits to the highest degree. We must also have religion and its moral resultant in the life of every citizen as a balance wheel to save the nation from moral collapse and final downfall. An ignorant crook will steal a ride; an educated crook will steal the railroad.

What of religion today? In 1895, Wilbur F. Crafts, in his *Practical Christian Sociology,* said:

> "From 1850 to 1870 the population gained 66 per cent, but evangelicals gained 89 per cent. From 1870 to 1880 population gained 30 per cent, evangelicals gained 50 per cent."

Following Dr. Craft's idea we compare the growth of church membership with that of population for ten-year periods beginning with 1870, the figures being from official sources.

POPULATION AND CHURCH GAIN

1870-1879	population gain	30	%,	church gain		50	%
1880-1889	"	"	25.5	%,	"	"	45	%
1890-1899	"	"	21	%,	"	"	40	%
1900-1909	"	"	20.7	%,	"	"	27	%
1910-1919	"	"	15	%,	"	"	22	%
1920-1929	"	"	16	%,	"	"	17	%
1930-1939	"	"	6.4	%,	"	"	6.1	%

The figures reveal that seventy years ago, and sixty years ago, the churches were on a triumphal march, gaining steadily on the population. Moreover it seemed that at no distant date the nation would be won for God. But that march has slowed down, and the gain of the churches on the population has been less and less until now the population is growing as fast as the churches, if not, indeed, faster, and no man can guess whether the churches are winning or losing in this land.

We churchmen dislike these figures. Even the veterans who gathered them seemed worried, for in transmitting the figures for 1930, 1932, and 1933, they sent long articles insisting that "the church is not dying," "the church has never lost ground," and "measure our back-to-the-church movement." We have the articles, and they do not explain. The figures stand, and we churchmen who know the facts weep and wonder what the figures mean. Even the *Christian Herald* that for long years published the figures has quit the task. One of the veteran church statisticians even boosted the membership figures ten million in a single year, and it would require but little study of the new figures to reveal an absurd situation. Now the statisticians seem troubled about which set of figures to use, the old or the new. But the proportionate increase is the same in either case. Using the new figures from 1932 to 1940, the churches have gained in membership less than six per cent, while the population for the same time has gained over six per cent. So figure as we may, the churches are not today keeping pace with the growth of the population.

The head of a great church educational institution recently attributed this slowing up of church growth to the law of diminishing returns. This law might apply in old communities where nearly all the people belong to some church, but such communities are rare in this country today. In a casual study of the subject in 1941, in five rural communities in New York, Ohio, and Indiana, the universal question asked us was: "How can we overcome religious

64

indifference?" When the church can no more than keep pace with the growing population, the church is failing. At best, that is the situation in this country today, and the sooner we churchmen find it out the better for us all.

Some brutal facts. The Methodists in the northern quarter of Illinois had 16,000 fewer pupils in Sunday school in 1941 than in 1921, a loss of 16 per cent. The United Presbyterian Church with 850 Sunday schools has lost 7,920 pupils in the last five years. The March 26, 1942, issue of the *Baptist Watchman-Examiner* named a certain great eastern city that now has "9,000 fewer Baptists than a few years ago." Another growing city formerly had thirteen Baptist churches where now "there are but five, and some of these are tottering." A rabbi speaking on the Jewish radio program not long ago is reported to have said, "The Jew in America has lost his religion." The Catholic Church reported a loss in membership in 1940. These are mere straws, but they note a general tendency and indicate the wind is blowing from a bad quarter.

Have our churches lost their militancy? Or

do they labor under difficulties they cannot overcome?

Unchurched children and youth. In 1920, the Inter-Church Movement surveyed the nation and reported that of 53 million children and youth, 37 million, seven in every ten, were unchurched. In 1926, the government investigated church school matters and reported a similar situation. There is a widespread call for later figures, but no reliable figures can be found. However, no man knowing the facts can believe that conditions have improved in the last twenty years. This is a most appalling situation that should have roused the nation long ago.

Personal experience. From 1920 to 1934, this writer was a virtual hobo, on the go seven days a week, speaking constantly in union meetings in many different cities and towns in forty states, working with many denominations, doing much personal investigation. Old church buildings were too large for present congregations. Sunday morning congregations were smaller than formerly. Children and youth were noticeably absent. Church doors were closed on Sunday night, or the old guard—a corporal's guard, the greyheads and the baldheads were holding the fort to stave off the curse of a churchless town on Sunday night. Midweek meetings were a thing of the past or a shadow of former greatness. Conditions were better in the South, but not encouraging there. Vast multitudes of city dwellers might as well live in Timbuctoo so far as being in touch with any church is concerned. No one contends that conditions have improved in the last ten years.

Churches not at fault. Many would lay the blame for all this upon the churches. But church equipment is the best ever and ministers never were better prepared or more aggressive for the kingdom than now. The truth is, the minister stands today with his back against a wall, fighting a defensive battle against the world, the flesh, and the devil. He and his helpers battle nobly but with small success against the appalling religious indifference, spiritual illiteracy, and widespread pagan influences of our day. In the minds of vast multitudes, religion is of minor importance, if, indeed, it has any value. It is our conviction that the absence of religion from our public schools for nearly three-quarters of a century is the main cause of this uphill struggle of the churches and of the growth of crime.

Secondary Causes

No one can say that the above picture is over-drawn or not according to the facts. No one can deny but that the condition pictured above is exactly what the prophets of the first chapter said it would be. Yet many offer other causes than the above for present-day crime and the struggle of the churches, and fairness requires us to evaluate these.

The war, say some, meaning the first World War, is the cause. War always increases crime and hurts religion. Wets blame the Eighteenth Amendment. Many blame the depression. Crime-breeding motion pictures are widely held to be a great cause of our ills. Two years active membership on the Chicago Motion Picture Censorship Commission appointed by the Chicago City Council convinced me that bad pictures are a tremendous urge to crime and nonreligion. Many blame immigration for the troubles we consider.

Others urge congestion in great cities. Some blame the new temptations of recent years. Breakdown of the homes and failure of the churches are twin charges widely hurled at us. These and many more are urged as producing the crime problem. No doubt these have helped to aggravate the condition. But are they the primary cause? The presence of the crime wave long before most of these were in existence effectively answers the charge.

Proof in Reverse

Refer again to the dicta of Benjamin Kidd, John H. Finley, and Henry L. Smith noted in the first chapter that what you put into the schools will in a generation dominate the nation, and what you drop from the schools will in a generation leave the nation. Religion left the schools in the '70's, and in 1890, crime was seen to be growing and religion suffering, just as the dicta said, just as the prophets declared. If a rule will not work in reverse, it may well be doubted. If it works both ways, it is pretty reliable, bears a strong stamp of truth. That is, if crime grows and religion suffers when religion leaves education, crime

69

should decline and religion flourish when religion returns to education, allowing in each case a few years to take effect. Is there evidence that such is the fact?

As to religion no evidence is obtainable.

Touching crime, there is some evidence, though it is too meager to satisfy a doubting Thomas. No state now teaches religion in the schools as in the old days. Only twelve states now read the Bible daily in all schools, and only a few of these have had the custom long enough to satisfy Mr. Kidd's dictum. Massachusetts has read the Bible daily in all schools since 1855. New York City has always used the Book in her schools daily and it has always been out of upstate schools. Pennsylvania schools have read the Scriptures every day to all children since 1913. Tennessee has had the law since 1915 and New Jersey since 1916.

A child's school life covers about ten years. Thus in the twenty-five years or more that the laws have been in effect in the above sections, more than two lots of children have gone clear through those schools. Granting that some reading is "perfunctory," granting that such small dosage is much less than children should receive, can any thoughtful person believe that listening to a Bible passage every morning for ten years would have no good result in the character of the average child? Or that there would be no cumulative benefit to successive generations of children? Can anyone deny that the more widespread the habit, the more improvement in the moral and religious character of the people? Or that quitting the practice would injure public religious and moral life? Perhaps now we can see how dropping the Bible hurt morals and religion as claimed by the wise far-seeing men quoted in the first chapter, and as shown by the statistics of crime and religion already given. It may be we can now see also how retaining or restoring the Bible-reading practice to the schools would tend to improve, or at least retard the decline of morals and religion; that is, prove the case in reverse, as indicated by the statistics given below.

Statistics from the Department of Commerce reveal that while crime increased 66.3 per cent over the nation from 1910 to 1938, it increased notably less in the five states with the Book in their schools for a period of twenty-five years or more—only 20 per cent in Massachusetts, 23 per cent in New York State, 16 per cent in New Jersey, 42 per cent in Pennsylvania, and 30 per cent in Tennessee. And this slight increase is in face of the fact, as everyone knows, that the first four of the above-named states are as wide open to all possible criminal tendencies as any other state in the union, if, indeed, not more so. Why, for example, should the war, or the depression, or bad movies, or congestion, or any other cause be less effective in hurting the morals of the young in these states than over the nation generally? Can it be that the children in these states receive at school some vitamin that makes them more immune to the moral ills of the day than those in other sections of the country?

Comparisons between different states can only be approximately correct, and to be at all fair, must be between states as nearly similarly situated as possible. No other states can be compared with the first four above named as well as those just west, and in these the growth of crime from 1910 to 1938 was as follows: 157.5 per cent in Ohio, 51.5 per cent in Indiana, 237 per cent in Illinois, 167.6 per cent in Michigan, 154 per cent in Iowa. Why was the growth of crime so much greater in these last named states which have no law requiring daily Bible reading in their schools than in those first noted? Again in 1910, crime was considerably less in the last five states than in the first four, but in 1938, it was very much greater. With practically every normal advantage in their favor the last named states make a much worse showing than the first named states. Why? The only true explanations are: (1) That what is called by many the main causes of our crime are at most but secondary causes, as claimed above. (2) That the daily Bible reading in all the schools of the first group of states and absent from the schools of the last named states really made the difference in crime. Moreover, any test you please can be made with any one of the states with the Bible in the schools named above and almost any other state in the union, and the result will favor the state with the Book of God before the children daily.

From the lack of longer time and wider and more intensive use of the Book in the schools, this test in reverse may not be considered proof by some, but if any man denies this, it is up to him to present a more satisfactory explanation of the facts presented.

To Sum Up

From this brief study of the nation today, the evidence seems abundantly sufficient that the men quoted in the first chapter were not false prophets, but wise, far-seeing statesmen, prophets of God, whose words are words of wisdom; that the absence of religion from our public schools is the underlying cause of our crime and irreligion; and that to save the nation from moral and religious collapse we must restore God to the public schools.

V

SUBSTITUTES FOR RELIGIOUS PUBLIC EDUCATION

Opponents of religion in public schools offer other methods of reaching the same end, and these proposals must be considered.

Religious Training in Home and Church

At one of my meetings a man asked, "Why don't you quit hitting schools and go after parents and churches?" I replied: "We will gladly do as you suggest if you will tell how any power on earth can compel any man to train his child aright or send him to church." That was ten years ago, and the question is still unanswered. More than that, as noted in Chapter I, multitudes of parents cannot and other multitudes will not train their children aright.

Also as we shall see in the next chapter, when the fathers gave us religious liberty and separation of church and state, they necessarily put beyond the power of the state to compel any child to go to church or to compel any church to train any child. All churches bid for the children and try to get them, but must depend upon voluntary attendance, and two-thirds of the children of the land forget the church. It is a beautiful vision to see all children flocking to the churches, but it is a delusion, a mirage. Knowing the truth, too wise to leave the nation depending for its life upon home and church, the fathers built the public school, made a religious program to fit the need, and required all children to attend school. In that 1847 report Horace Mann said the program would meet the need. For many years it did meet the need, and the nation prospered.

Then came the day when, covertly, with no change of law, religion and morals were crowded out of schools. Very soon after that, came the decline of morals and the growth of crime until now we are the most lawless of nations. Then came also the struggle of the churches against increasing odds until the victorious stride of the past is gone and the churches battle to hold their own.

Now come those who, unaware of our history and of the relative power of schools and churches, insist that the state is secular and must not teach religion in the schools and that the task belongs only to homes and churches. All good citizens gladly hold that homes and churches should do all possible to promote religion and good morals. Every informed man knows that there are millions of children whom the churches cannot reach, also that multitudes of children have incompetent or neglectful parents, or are victims of broken homes. Where can these get the necessary training for good citizenship if not in the public schools? Finally what psychological, what pedagogical folly to feed the poison of secularism, practical atheism, in the schools and expect the antidote to be applied in home and church!

The Jewish Suggestion

Like all religious people, Jews hold that "the ultimate sanction of morality is religion, and that religious training is essential to good citizenship." In 1926, the Joint Commission of Religious Education of the Union of American Hebrew Congregations and Central Conference of American Rabbis said that they were "opposed to any form of religious instruction as part of the public school system or during school hours." They said: "We advocate that public schools reduce their time schedule by closing the entire public school system one hour or more at the end of the school day. The time thus put at the disposal of children may be used by the parents for such instruction of their children as they see fit."[1] This seems to be the position of Jews generally.

In saying "religious training is essential to good citizenship" they start well. But in taking the above position they cut the ground from under their own feet. *To say that a nation must not do the thing necessary to her own life is to deny sovereignty and admit that the nation is only a weakling.*

Their suggestion is too puerile to come from such wise people as the Jews.

See the plan they suggest. They would close all schools an hour early and give the time to parents to train their children as they see fit. They do not explain the alchemy by which parents not interested in religion for their children at four o'clock would be interested at three o'clock. They do not explain how the two-thirds of American children who now receive no religious training would get it if let out of school an hour earlier. *The plan simply amounts to letting the children of the nation out of school for an hour more of play and temptation upon the street.* Please note, too, that the Jewish plan opposes released-time, week-day church schools.

The Parochial School

Roman Catholics, Missouri Synod Lutherans, Christian Reformed, and Seventh Day Adventists, when possible, build parochial schools and make religion a vital part of the program. All other Christian groups in the land patronize public schools. The four groups above, as groups, strongly oppose religion in public schools, and they alone of Christian groups take that stand. They oppose the public school as "godless" and take their children out and still insist upon keeping the schools "godless." When they take their children out of the state schools and at great expense build schools of their own, we incline to commend their religious devotion. But when, with their children gone, they still fight to keep the public schools "godless," we wonder quite a bit at their supposed superior religious devotion. Why do they still oppose God in the schools when their own children are absent? Are they more patriotic than the rest of us? Do they have a deeper insight into fundamental American principles than we? Do they thus invite us to set up parochial schools and thus weaken or destroy our public school system? Do they seek some sectarian advantage? Let them explain.

Can the parochial schools solve the problem of religion in education? Never. Even if all other churches followed suit and set up parochial schools there would still be in the sadly weakened public school the two-thirds of the children who never darken church doors, and from these would still come the dangerous elements we now have.

Released-time Weekday Church Schools

Starting in Gary, Indiana, in 1914, such schools now exist in thirty-eight states. The aim is to have children excused from school one or two hours a week to attend religious instruction classes elsewhere under church control and at church expense. Its leaders are Protestants with a few Catholics, and they are very aggressive. When promoting their plan, they assume a superior air and mildly assert (as positively as if it came direct from heaven), "Of course separation of church and state forbids the state to teach religion." They refuse to debate. You cannot drag them into argument.

There is a great literature on the subject and much publicity, but the number of schools is surprisingly small for nearly thirty years' effort. Bulletin No. 3 on the subject issued in July, 1941, by the U. S. Office of Education says that 488 of such schools were reported over the nation in 1940 with an average daily attendance of 135,877. It adds that there was probably an increase of nineteen per cent in the number of schools since 1932, but that "more than half of the programs reported in 1932 have either discontinued the program or the program has created too little interest to prompt a reply to a survey inquiry." The public does not seem to be sold on the idea. What of the plan? But two features are considered here, both fatally faulty.

1. **It cannot solve the nation's moral and**

religious problem, that of making good citizens of the two-thirds of the children that never darken church doors. The plan must depend upon voluntary attendance, and it is folly to think that those who will not go to church school on Sunday will go on Friday. It is also folly to think that where churches cannot live, week-day church schools can live. Hence, such schools cannot reach the millions in unchurched rural communities, nor the multitudes in blighted sections of great cities, nor the other throngs everywhere who pass up the church school on Sunday. Thus, say what its advocates will, these schools can in the main give only a little more religious training to those who in Sunday school already receive some, while leaving untouched the vast throngs that need it most —those from whom come the problem child and criminal adult. Three examples tell the story.

There is not a finer town in America to illustrate the value of the weekday church school in reaching the children than Oak Park, Illinois, just outside of Chicago. This is a city of over 60,000 people, almost purely American and Protestant, very wealthy, with many fine churches, which has had a weekday church school held up as a model for many years. On March 18, 1941, the superintendent of Oak Park schools wrote me there were 5,077 pupils enrolled in elementary schools, and of these 1,600 were being excused for instruction in weekday church schools, considerably fewer than a third.

More recent figures from Gary, Indiana, where the plan has been in operation many years show fewer than a fifth of the public school children in the weekday church schools.

Virginia is held up as a fine example of what weekday church schools can do. I wrote for information and on February 24, 1941, received a reply from the state superintendent of these schools. The church schools there are fifteen years old, and from enclosures and federal statistics I garnered the figures, 28,627 in church schools last year, one in twenty of the children of school age in the state—twice as many babies born every year as the total enrollment in these schools. The superintendent was proud of the 28,627 in his schools, but I thought of the 531,000 not in their schools and wondered at what date the church schools could catch up with the growth of the school population. I asked about colored schools, and he *hoped* they had some church schools. I also asked about schools in rural sections, and he *hoped* they, too, had some.

Judging from the above examples, the ship of state will be hopelessly wrecked long before help can arrive from that source. Advocates admit that many communities try the plan and fail, and we can name men formerly enamored of the plan who now see differently.

2. **It is built upon a fatally faulty and dangerous foundation.** Before us lies the "Announcement of the Twenty-Fourth Annual Convention of the Religious Education Association, April 26-29, 1927," held in Chicago. The last page is devoted wholly to the released-time, weekday church school. Two sentences stand out: "Because of the secular nature of the state, its schools may not teach religion, nor can any appeal be made to religious motive," and this: "Religious motivation may not be used—the name of God may not be used." Many educational leaders from both church and state in this country and Canada were on the program. I heard every word. Only Dr. Luther

Weigle mentioned the above words and said, "I was amazed," and after quoting the words, added:

> "The error of this statement lies in its seeming to assert as a necessary principle what is unfortunately, in too many sections of the country, the fact."[2]

After the convention I sent letters to every man on the program and some others, sixty in all, asking if they agreed with the sentiment. Thirty replied, mostly public schoolmen, and every man said, "No." Released-timers did not reply. The words are simply astounding. If they be true, both the nation and the weekday school will perish, killed by the righteous wrath of an indignant God. But the words are false. How they could come from a clear brain is hard to comprehend.

The position of released-timers is less defensible than that of parochial school promoters. Both say the public school is "godless." The latter try to get their children out of the poisonous atmosphere. The former are willing for the poison to work on all the children twenty-nine hours a week if they can apply the antidote to a few of them one hour a week.

Nonreligious Morals in Public Schools

Some secular groups advocate such teaching in the schools. Religion excluded, there are many systems of morals—hedonistic, utilitarian, intuitionist, behaviorist, and what not. From Plato to John Dewey, no two moral philosophers agree on what is right or wrong. Buddha taught you must not kill anything. Plato taught his followers to kill unfavored babies. Nietzsche cries, "Kill, kill, for war is the highest and noblest occupation of humans." So with many doctors of many schools, just what ethical concoction shall be prescribed for school children? And how often would the prescription be changed by warring doctors?

Some suggest the ethics of Jesus, minus Jesus. This is plagiarism. It makes stealing the basis of ethics, insults the greatest teacher of the race, and makes clever crooks.

Educational leaders hold that character building is the highest aim of all education. The laws of the states are all but unanimous in requiring that morals be taught in public schools. Still there is very little moral training in the schools today. A professor in an Illinois teachers' college said, "We teach morals in our college," and won the reply, "Good, what text do you use?" He answered, "We depend upon the occasional remark of the teacher," and the query went back, "Do you teach mathematics or history that way?" Two teachers in Jackson, Michigan, said, "You are mistaken; we teach morals in our rooms." When asked to specify, they stumbled a bit and at last said, "We teach children to say 'please,' 'thank you,' 'excuse me,' 'good morning.' " The reply went back, "That is not morals, but manners." An Indiana teacher said, "I teach 'Thou shalt not kill' and 'Thou shalt not steal,' " and was asked, "Do you teach, God says, 'Thou shalt not kill'?" The reply came quickly, "Oh, no, we must not say that."

The Bible left the Chicago schools in 1884. In 1920, churchmen found that there was no systematic moral training in the schools and asked the school board to do something about it. They did. The resulting pamphlet combed all literature, the Bible excluded, for stories of moral intent to tell the children. Today even that is gone, and nothing takes its place.

Two duds. Some years ago, The Character

Education Association, of Washington, D. C., gave two prizes for the best codes of morals to use with the young, *religion excluded.* In 1916, it gave $5,000 for the best code of morals for elementary school children. A little later it gave $20,000 for the best code to use in public schools, and Prof. E. D. Starbuck and a group of Iowa teachers won the prize. Both codes are on my desk, and they contain no more God, Bible, Ten Commandments, Golden Rule, etc., than if these did not exist. Both fell as duds. The organization is gone, and the codes are gone.

For years I was on the mailing list of the Federal Office of Education, and many documents reached me on educational matters. The curricula of normal colleges were scanned. Many textbooks on pedagogy were examined. In all this there was almost nothing on moral training in the schools. All else under the stars, but very little of this, the most important of all. Plenty to sharpen the wits but little to strengthen the character. There was not even a textbook to put into the hands of a teacher. And even teachers who try to teach morals admitted that their efforts are "indefinite and unorganized" and "moving by no special plan toward nowhere in particular," as Prof. Starbuck declared after two extensive investigations.

This is not a criticism, but almost a compliment to the teachers. They are religious and know that morals cannot be taught except upon a religious foundation. And with the Bible gone from the schools, morals are gone and cannot be taught.

Churches teach Christian morals. Put anything else in the schools and there would be endless conflict between church and school. Hear Dr. Weigle again:

> "If the state in the public school must teach that right is merely what men have agreed on, and nothing more than public opinion, if they are stopped from saying that some things are right because we believe them rooted in the constitution of the universe itself, expressions of the nature and will of God, then we are in the presence of a new danger. Shall the state teach that right is mere fashion, and the church that it has the stamp of eternity? That would be a conflict in the field of morality beside which the supposed conflict between evolution and Genesis is child's play."[3]

Finally man-made morals in the schools

mean no God in the schools. And that would mean a nation without God, and that means atheism, irreligion, crime, chaos, destruction.

Religion and Morals in Prisons

Several states quite indifferent to religion in the schools seem very insistent that religion must be in the prisons. May we insult good sense and ask if some such scheme would meet our need?

The Ohio prison law says, "The warden shall furnish each convict with a Bible." Bibles must also be given to all inmates of jails. Like other states Ohio doubtless employs ministers as chaplains to give convicts moral and religious instruction. If Ohio had put the Bible into all her public schools in 1913, as her neighbor, Pennsylvania, did, with the same result, more than half of her present 9,310 convicts would now be law-abiding citizens and the state would be saving the $1,550,000 a year that it costs to house and feed them.

Illinois prison law. "It shall be the duty of the chaplains to perform religious services in the penitentiaries, to attend to the spiritual wants of the convicts, to visit the convicts in their cells for the purpose of giving them moral and religious instruction, and to furnish, at the expense of the state, a Bible to each convict." But in 1910, by a vote of five to two, the State Supreme Court held that the Bible has no right in the schools of the state.

Michigan prison law. "The chaplain shall hold religious services in the prison, and he shall attend to the spiritual wants of the convicts, he shall give the convicts moral and religious instruction, and he shall, at the expense of the state, furnish a Bible to each convict." But in 1929, and since, the legislature has feared to tell schoolteachers to read the Bible to children at school.

Washington State Constitution. "No public money shall be applied to any religious worship, exercise, or instruction." In 1904, by popular vote the constitution was amended to provide chaplains to give convicts moral and religious instruction. But the attorney general said there should be no Bible in the public schools, and in 1918, the State Supreme Court forbade schoolteachers to give credit for Bible study even if the study be done out of school hours and school buildings.

What is true of the above states as to Bibles and religious instruction in prison is true over the nation. Bibles are furnished with or without law, and chaplains are paid by the state to give convicts moral and religious instruction. In many prisons convicts must attend church on Sunday.

Don't we have sense enough to know we are going at this thing wrong? Bibles kept away from school children and put into the hands of convicts delight devils and drive us straight toward the jungle.

No Substitute for God in the Schoolhouse

All the above suggestions miss the issue. The real problem is not how we sectarians may get a few more children for our church, not how we may give a little more religious instruction to those who now have some. The real problem is, how can the two-thirds of the children of the land whom the churches cannot reach be given such moral and religious instruction as will help them to become good citizens rather than crooks, radicals, and prison birds? It is not a sectarian, but a religious, moral, and patriotic problem.

Four facts should now be evident to thinking people: (1) No plan mentioned above is now solving nor can solve the problem; (2) If, or when, ruin comes from secular education, no creed will be exempt; we will all sink in the common ruin; (3) Our only safety is in restoring God to His empty throne in the schoolrooms of the land; (4) With the truths of religion accepted by all Christians restored to the schools, matters cannot be worse and would certainly be better for us all—Jew and Gentile, Catholic and Protestant. That is the thought of the men quoted in the first chapter. That would seem to be the wise view for us all.

If the fundamental principles of this government do not now permit religion in the school house, those principles must be changed. Let us examine the principles.

REFERENCES

1. Religious Education Journal, June, 1927. pp. 590-591.
2. Ibid., p. 575.
3. Ibid., pp. 578-579.

VI

FUNDAMENTAL PRINCIPLES

The question of the right of religion in public education involves three fundamental principles of our government: religious liberty, separation of church and state, and national sovereignty. No discussion of the subject of this book would be complete without a consideration of these three principles.

The war-torn world and our madly mounting crime wave warn that without religion to restrain, direct, and uplift, man is a bloodthirsty beast, dragging humanity straight to the jungle. They also warn that the recent vast increase of mental training demands a like increase of moral training to save the beast from becoming more dangerous. There being no other way to do it, the state that now whets the brain of every child must also give to every child the religious training that will make him a safe citizen. If our present principles of religious liberty, separation of church and state, and national sovereignty forbid such training in the public schools, then, to save civilization, we must change the principles.

Note. *The intent of the lawmaker is the law.* This is a basic rule well-known to lawyers, but little known to laymen. Not your notion nor mine, but what did the makers of the law mean by it. Otherwise laws would change with the wind or the notions of folks. What a law meant to those who made it, that it always means until properly changed by properly constituted authorities.

Religious Liberty

Roger Williams, the founder of the Baptist Church in America, was the first to demand liberty of conscience, or religious liberty, on the shores of America. What did he mean by liberty of conscience? In 1655, he wrote a letter to the town of Providence, defining the term by use of a parable:

> "There goes many a ship to sea, with many hundred souls in one ship, whose weal and woe is common, and it is a true picture of a commonwealth, or human combination, or society. It hath fallen out sometimes that both Papists and Protestants,

Jews and Turks may be embarked on the same
ship; upon which proposal I affirm that all the liberty of conscience I ever pleaded for, turns upon
these two hinges, that none of the Protestants,
Papists, Jews or Turks be forced to come to the
ship's prayers or worship, nor be compelled from
their own particular prayers or worship, if they
practice any."[1]

This gives no comfort to those who think
religious liberty shuts God out of the school
house. The ship has prayers. Those who wish
attend and others are absent. And the right to
have prayers carries with it the right to employ
those willing to conduct prayers and to use the
ship's money to pay the bills. But the ship is the
state, and this leaves the state not secular but
religious, actually having prayers, not merely
granting the right to have them. Put in terms of
the school, the school has prayers, employs
teachers willing to conduct prayers, pays for
them with school money, permits those who wish
to be present, and allows others to be absent.
The founder of the American Baptist Church
was a wise statesman who built a religious state
but compelled nobody to conform. He asked
liberty *to* worship for those who wished to wor-

ship, and liberty *not* to worship for those who preferred not to do so. That is liberty for all, and what is not liberty for all is not liberty at all.

But suppose some of the "Papists, Jews, or Turks" want prayers of their own, as Williams suggested? Let them have them, of course, just as we now do in prison and army. They will be better citizens for it, and that is what we want.

The Virginia Struggle

Virginia was the leading state in those days; the great battle for religious liberty was fought there, and the victory spread over the land. The Church of England was established; all had to pay taxes to support it; many disabilities were forced upon dissenters, and some militant ministers were imprisoned. Presbyterians and a few Baptists came about 1690 and objected mildly but yielded. About 1740, Separatist Baptists came and battled hard against all restrictions. In 1770, the battle was hot to remove all restrictions and make all churchmen equal before the law. Presbyterians and Baptists fought side by side. Other denominations had few members. Authorities needed help from dissenters in the approaching struggle with England, and began to sympathize. Every semiannual session of the legislature was flooded with petitions, and strong lobbies were there from both dissenting groups. In 1775, a convention was called to draft a new constitution. Strong lobbies were there and many petitions. In 1776, a new constitution was adopted, and this contained the now famous Section 16 of the Bill of Rights that stands today, still the same number. Patrick Henry probably wrote the words, and to him, not to Jefferson, belongs the credit of being the father of religious liberty in Virginia. Long before Jefferson appeared, Henry was in the courts of the state, defending and advising, without pay, the militant Baptists, and he was their champion all the way through. Section 16 said:

> "That religion, or the duty we owe our Creator, and the manner of discharging it, can be directed only by reason and conviction, not by force or violence; and therefore all men are equally entitled to the free exercise of religion according to the dictates of conscience; and it is the highest duty of all to practice Christian forbearance, love and charity toward each other."

This is one of the greatest and least known sentences in American history. In sixty-five words Virginia did five things that became standard for the nation and that live today in all the land: (1) Defined religion. (2) Granted religious liberty. (3) Asserted her own liberty of religion. (4) Announced her religious choice —Christianity. (5) Proclaimed her moral standard. The above definition of religion was used by the Federal Supreme Court in 98 U. S. 145, thus making it the legal definition of religion in this country.

To effectuate Section 16, in 1779, Jefferson introduced into the Virginia legislature what became his famous statute of religious liberty. It was passed in 1785, James Madison being then its sponsor. Henry was governor, and Jefferson was in Europe. The bill was called "A Bill for the Establishment of Religious Freedom." After the preamble it said:

"Be it enacted by the General Assembly, that no man shall be compelled to frequent or support any religious worship, place or ministry whatsoever, nor shall he be enforced, restrained, molested or burthened in body or goods, nor shall otherwise suffer on account of his opinions in matters of religion,

and that the same shall in no wise diminish, enlarge
or affect their civil status."

The adoption of this bill ended the century-
long conflict. Religious liberty and separation
of church and state were complete in Virginia.
To be exact, they mean the same thing except
that the first is the root while the last is the
necessary fruit.

*Observe that the law was not forced upon
unwilling churchmen by atheists and infidels,
as often charged, but that Christian churchmen
began the fight, pushed the battle and maintained it with full vigor until victory came.
Observe, too, that Christian churchmen were
legislative leaders for liberty—Patrick Henry,
probably a Presbyterian; James Madison, an
Episcopalian, educated for the pulpit; and
Thomas Jefferson, a devout Episcopalian, a
Unitarian, deeply religious, as the Declaration
of Independence, from his pen, reveals.*

Religious Liberty Defined

We find no exact definition, but the Statute
of Religious Freedom points to the meaning
when it says, in the preamble:

"To suffer the civil magistrate to intrude his

powers into the field of opinion, and to restrain the profession or propagation of principles on the supposition of their evil tendency, is a dangerous fallacy which at once destroys all religious liberty. It is enough for the rightful purposes of civil government for its officials to interfere when principles break out into overt acts against peace and good order."

Jefferson wrote the words. Some years later, just after Congress adopted the first amendment to the Federal Constitution, he wrote a letter to the Danbury Baptist Association and set forth the limits of religious liberty in these words: "A man has no natural right in opposition to his social duties."[2] About eighty years later, when the Federal Supreme Court held that Congress could prohibit the practice of polygamy, the Court quoted these words of Jefferson with approval and made them the basis of the decision against polygamy, and said:

"Congress was left free to reach actions which were in violation of social duties or subversive of good order."—98 U. S. 145.

Later, in 186 U. S. 393, the same high Court said:

"For the public good, individuals must suffer the destruction of property or even life, rights, of necessity, being parts of that law, and the possession and enjoyment of all rights are subject to such reasonable conditions as may be decreed by the governing authority essential to safety, health, peace, good order and morals of the community."

These words agree perfectly with Jefferson's statement in the preamble. Thus *religious liberty is the right to believe and preach as one sees fit and to practice one's belief within the limits of public welfare.*

Plainly one's religious liberty ends with his own person. There is nothing here to permit one to veto the Bible in the public schools because he does not want his child to hear it read. A man's right ends with his having his child excused from taking part in the service. This leaves no man free to oppose religion in army, navy, courts, legislature, schools, or other public functions. It only permits him to be excused from the service. That is the Roger Williams' idea, Jefferson's idea, the American idea.

Separation of Church and State Defined

We find no verbal definition of separation of church and state, but the practice of the fathers shows what they meant. There is no hint that they intended to make a secular state, a political atheism, with no right to use or promote religion, as claimed by those who oppose religion in the schools. There is indeed much to the contrary. During the hundred years' strife, they had daily prayers in the legislature, chaplains in the army, religion in the schools, with no voice lifted against them. Moreover they remained after these years of strife the same as before. In fact one of the Baptist demands was that they be given chaplaincies in the army on the same basis as the Episcopalians. Had the question ever been raised, those battling Baptists and Presbyterians would have denied with hot indignation that they sought to make a secular state. And *Virginia Baptists today must cease their opposition to the Bible in the schools or charge their forbears with religious heresy.* As a moral person Virginia did change its religion. It had been Episcopalian. It became Christian with no denominational tag, and it remains so to this day. In 1922, the State Supreme Court (114 S. E. 764) spoke as follows:

"From the creation of the state until the present

time this state has been recognized as a Christian state. It will be observed that while there was a direct purpose to sever church and state and to give fullest freedom of conscience and to abolish tithes and spiritual courts there was no assault upon Christianity or any other religious faith. Indeed constitutional provisions enjoin the practice of Christian forbearance, love and charity. The framers of these laws knew then, as we know now, that we are a Christian people, that the morality of the state is deeply grafted upon Christianity."

The court was defending the right of the state to make and enforce laws forbidding Sunday labor, and it upheld the laws on the ground that Sunday labor is repugnant to the sentiment of a Christian state. Thus Virginia did not become secular in 1776. She did not become indifferent or inimical to religion. She had been favoring one church and penalizing others. She simply took her hands off all churches and agreed in future to treat all alike and to retain her own right to maintain and promote nonsectarian religon.

There was one necessary implicit restriction, noted by Jefferson, on both church and state. This restriction is to be found in the preamble quoted above and in the setting up of the University of Virginia, to be considered later. It provides that the church may do nothing inimical to public welfare and the state may use only such religious doctrines as are acceptable to Christian groups generally. *Thus separation of church and state means that the two are different institutions, neither with any right to control the other in matters religious, except that no church practice may injure the public and that the state may not foster any religious doctrines on which Christian sects differ, the state—all the people—being the judge in both instances.*

The Virginia Idea in the Federal Constitution

The Virginia struggle ended in 1785. In 1787, the Federal Constitution was written and submitted to the states. In Virginia, then the leading state, the battle was fierce. Washington and Madison, who helped to make the Constitution, were for it, and Madison was a candidate for membership in the next Congress, the first under the new document. Jefferson, in Europe, favored. Henry opposed. Militant Baptists were roused, and put a strong candidate in the field against Madison, the main ground of the opposition being lack of clarity in the new document on religious liberty. Virginia was a pivot state. Opposition subsided. The candidate opposing Madison withdrew, apparently on condition that Madison, in no uncertain words, would submit to Congress a proposal granting religious liberty. The amendment, probably written by Henry, was introduced by Madison and adopted by Congress as part of the first amendment to the new Constitution, and all were satisfied. There was no debate in Congress as to the meaning of the words. Several said they wanted to guard the rights of conscience and religion, "but not patronize those who professed no religion." Madison explained what he meant by the words.[3] Coming as it did from Virginia, with Madison, Jefferson, Henry, and the church people of the state back of it, it must have meant the same as the words they had just put into their own constitution: "Congress shall make no law respecting an establishment of religion, or prohibiting the free exercise thereof." Those are the words, and they stand today unchanged. They control Congress only, no state; yet in a short time, the other states fell into line and religious liberty, separation of church and state, became the universal law of the land.

Judge Story on the Constitution

In his *"Constitution,"* written in 1833, speaking of the first amendment, Judge Story said:

"The promulgation of the great doctrines of religion, the being, and attributes, and providence of Almighty God; the responsibility to Him for all our actions, founded upon moral freedom and accountability, the future state of rewards and punishment, the cultivation of all personal, social and benevolent virtues—these can never be a matter of indifference to any well-ordered community. It is indeed difficult to conceive how any civilized society can exist without them, and at all events, it is impossible for those who believe in the truth of Christianity as a divine revelation to doubt it is a special duty of government to foster and encourage it among all citizens and subjects. This is a matter wholly distinct from that of the right of private judgment in matters of religion, and of matters of public worship according to the dictates of one's own conscience."—Section 1811.

"Probably at the time of the adoption of the constitution and the amendment now under consideration, the general, if not the universal, sentiment in America was that Christianity ought to receive encouragement from the state so far as it was not in conflict with the private right of conscience and freedom of religious worship. An attempt to level all religions, and to make it a matter of state policy to hold all in utter indifference, would have created universal disapprobation, if not universal indignation."—Section 1874.

"The real object of the amendment was not to countenance, much less to advance, Mohammedanism, or Judaism, or infidelity, by prostituting Christianity; but to exclude all rivalry between Christian sects."—Section 1877.

The National Congress

In the thirty-second and thirty-third Congresses a strong effort was made to abolish the office of chaplains in army, navy, and the two houses of Congress. The effort failed, and on March 27, 1853, the House of Representatives said this in a resolution:

"Had the people, during the Revolution, had a suspicion of any attempt to war against Christianity, that revolution would have been strangled in its cradle. At the time of the adoption of the constitution and its amendments, the universal sentiment was that *Christianity* should be encouraged, not any one sect. Any attempt to level or discard all religion would have been viewed with universal indignation. The object was not to substitute Judaism, or Mohammedanism, or infidelity, but to prevent rivalry among sects to the exclusion of others."[4]

Ordinance of 1787

This is one of the most notable laws ever passed by representatives of the American people. Passed by the last Continental Congress, it was accepted in 1789 by the first Federal Congress, and controlled the territory between Pennsylvania and the Mississippi and north of the Ohio River. Our interest is in the words: "RELIGION, MORALITY AND KNOWLEDGE, BEING NECESSARY TO GOOD GOVERNMENT AND THE HAPPINESS OF MANKIND, SCHOOLS AND THE MEANS OF EDUCATION SHALL FOREVER BE ENCOURAGED." These words are the MAGNA CHARTA of our public school system. The Ordinance was written by Nathan Dane who was born, reared, and educated in Massachusetts, and who became one of the most celebrated jurists of that state. Religion has always been in the schools of that state, and Mr. Dane knew nothing else than religion in the schoolhouse. The words speak authoritatively on the *importance,* the *purpose,* and the *content of public education.* As to importance, "necessary"; as to purpose, "good government and the happiness of mankind"; as to content, "religion, morality and knowledge." *By no rule of logic or law can the words be construed to give religion less right in public education than secular knowledge.* Dane knew nothing else. The people of that day in Congress knew nothing else. The *Ordinance also established religious liberty in this great Northwest Territory, thus showing that religious liberty and religion in the schoolhouse are not antagonistic principles.*

A Sovereign Christian Nation

"This Is a Christian Nation." This is the crux of the whole matter. Is Uncle Sam an atheist? Or a secularist? Or a Christian? Legal minds say a state is a "moral person" with as much power and right of choice as any human being. France chose to be secular; Italy, Roman Catholic; Sweden, Lutheran. What of Uncle Sam? The Federal Constitution is silent. If any member of the convention knew French secularism, it was Benjamin Franklin, who did not want it.

He urged daily prayers in the convention, but failed—not from secularist influence, but from fear of sectarian strife, which was bitter in those days. God is not recognized in the document. It was a big mistake, but they were praying men and got their ideas of government from God's Book. In the famous Trinity Church case (143 U. S. 457), the Federal Supreme Court examined our nation's background, laws, customs, moral standards, and said: "THIS IS A CHRISTIAN NATION"—not as an aside, an *obiter dictum,* but as the hinge on which the case swung. In the Girard Will case in 1844 (2 Howard U. S. 200), after listening to the matchless argument by Daniel Webster that the will was void because placing conditions repugnant to this Christian nation, the Court sustained the will, and said, "Why may not the Bible—and especially the New Testament—be read and taught?" and made this the fact on which to decide the case. While this was a private school, the Court tacitly admitted Webster's contention that this is a Christian nation. Many state supreme courts have said the same for their states: New York, Pennsylvania, Virginia, Illinois, Iowa, New Jersey, etc. No,

Uncle Sam is not an atheist, nor a secularist, but a Christian. Sad to say, he has adopted some pagan practices, and must get right with God by restoring religion to the schools or perish through secularism and crime.

This Nation Is Sovereign

In brief, the right of all the people acting as one for the good of all and each—that is sovereignty. The right to defend itself, to promote the common good—this is a fundamental, inalienable right of any state, a right that it cannot give up and live. In 1860, the Mormon Church believed in, preached and its members practiced polygamy as a religious rite. The government said, "Stop." Mormons refused and continued the practice under the plea of religious liberty. A thirty-year war followed. Mormons evaded every prohibition. They were fined, imprisoned, the church dissolved, church property confiscated, their leaders in hiding. The Federal High Court sustained every move of government on the ground that "religious liberty does not permit immoral practices under the guise of religious worship" (98 U. S. 163). The Mormons promised to quit the practice, were forgiven, their property restored, and all appears to go well.[5] *A people who set up a government have an inalienable right to defend it.* That is why every man of us may be taken for cannon fodder. That right is expressed in army, navy, police, courts, prisons, schools, asylums, quarantine, etc. In Lawton versus Steele (152 U. S. 133), the Federal Supreme Court said of the police power: "It is generally conceded to include everything essential to public safety, health and morals." The Chicago City Council could not have stopped smoking on the street cars in twenty years, but the Board of Health, for the public good, stopped it in one short order. Let America once wake up to the fact that religionless public schools are breaking the nation through irreligion and crime, and something will happen. This nation is not a parasite— a feeble vine, clinging to and sucking its lifeblood from the church. This nation is sovereign. Like a sturdy oak, it is able to stand alone, drinking its lifeblood direct from God's illimitable supply. It took its hands off all individuals and churches in matters religious but limited religious liberty to conduct that does not injure the public. It exercised its own religious liberty and chose to be Christian with no sectarian bias, chose also to use its religion in its own functions. And it uses it now in army, navy, courts, legislatures, prisons—everywhere except in public schools. To preserve its own life, as it has adopted compulsory education so must it enthrone God in the public schoolrooms of the land.

To preserve and protect its own life, this sovereign nation has as much right to be religious and to use and foster religion as any man alive or any church within its borders. No law of God nor of this land denies that right. Only secularists and thoughtless churchmen deny it. To destroy that right is to turn us back to the jungle.

Corollaries

In this religious nation, it is axiomatic that religious training is essential to good citizenship. Bills of rights granted to individuals and groups are limitations of its power by a sovereign state. It is unthinkable that a sovereign state would so limit its power as to endanger its own life, for that would deny the very essence

114

of sovereignty. From the above axiom and the three principles of government under consideration—state sovereignty, religious liberty, and separation of church and state—certain corollaries may be deduced:

Religious training being essential to good citizenship, the state has a perfect right to find a way whereby such training may be given, otherwise the state would not be sovereign.

No church nor combination of churches may claim, nor may the state grant to homes and churches, the *exclusive* right to give such training, for that would destroy all the principles involved and risk the life of the nation.

There being no other way to *assure* the necessary training for all, the state is in duty bound to give such training herself. *This means that God must be in the public schools.*

The Duty of Home, Church, State

Religious character being for the highest good of all in all relations of life, the three institutions—home, church, and state—each having to do with child training, each sovereign in its own field, each has a right and a high duty to give to every child it can reach the best religious

115

training possible, regardless of what others may do. The task is big enough for the best efforts of all. They may co-operate. They should co-operate. They must never antagonize each other, for all rise or fall together. Thus only may our essential principles be preserved and the highest good of all be realized.

The Practice in Virginia Schools

In early days, Virginia did not have public schools like ours. Hers were parish schools, controlled by the church, in which poor children were educated at public expense, thus being practically public schools. During all the struggle for religious liberty, religion was in the schools, and it remained long after, just as before, with no word that it did not belong there.[6]

Illuminating events occurred in connection with the state university. Except on the basis of providential guidance, it is difficult to explain how the two men who, forty years before, had led the battle for religious liberty, were now the very men to set up the state university and apply in education the principles they had championed long before. Both men had been President. Both were old. Ordinarily younger men would have led the effort, but we find Jefferson and Madison at the task. In 1818, the legislature appointed a committee of twenty to draft a plan for the state university and submit a curriculum. Jefferson was chairman. He prepared the report which included this paragraph:

> "In conformity with the principles of our constitution, which places all sects of religion on an equal footing, we have proposed no professor of divinity; and the rather as the proofs of the being of God, the Creator, Preserver and Ruler of the universe, the author of all the relations of morality, and the laws and obligations these infer, will be within the province of the professor of ethics; to which adding the developments of those moral obligations, of those in which all sects agree, with a knowledge of the languages, Hebrew, Greek and Latin, a basis will be found common to all the sects. Proceeding thus far without offense to the constitution, we have thought it proper at this point to let every sect provide, as they think fittest, the means of further instruction in their own particular tenets."[7]

What could be plainer than the above, that in adopting religious liberty and separation of church and state, the state did not become secular? Especially when the words come from the very man accused of championing secularism? How could the need and place of religion in education be better shown? God must have preserved Jefferson to write that paragraph for our learning. The legislature passed the law just as suggested, appointed a committee of seven, called visitors, to set up the university, and Jefferson and Madison were members of the committee, with the former as chairman.

One of their first acts made trouble. They chose Thomas Cooper, a Unitarian, very brilliant, very liberal, as a professor. Presbyterians objected and charged that the committee sought to exclude all religion from the schools. Cooper was dismissed. In his next report, Jefferson hotly denied the charge and, at great length, showed that the committee was putting much religion into the institution, free from sectarianism. This report, with that before given the legislature by Jefferson, showed that state and church should co-operate in moral and religious training of youth and that the state had a duty of its own to that end. When the report appeared, Presbyterians were satisfied, criticism ceased, and religion was in the university, put there by the very men who forty years before led the battle for separation of church and state.[8]

How, and how much was religion in the institution? Jefferson was chosen Rector, that is, president and manager.[9] He planned the buildings and supervised their erection. He chose the motto of the University and had it engraved on the central building, the words of Jesus, "Ye shall know the truth and the truth shall make you free."[10] One of the buildings contained a chapel and a library. Of the first 1,500 books, 175 were on religion.[11] The library was to have the writings "of the most respected authorities of every sect," and "courses of ethical lectures were to be given at regular intervals for the education of students in those moral obligations in which all sects agree,"[12] i. e., with religious sanction. The different sects were invited to build schools for the training of ministers on the confines, or even on the grounds, and such students would have all privileges of the university free, "to make the general religion a religion of peace, reason and morality."[13] All students were to attend chapel daily.[14] Ethics with religious sanctions was a part of the regular course of study.[15] After the school was opened on March 7, 1825, prayers were held every evening in chapel, and regular religious services were held twice every Sunday led by ministers of different sects.[16] Lectures were given each term on religious and scriptural subjects—Bible History, Life of Christ, Life of St. Paul, etc.—sectarian matters omitted.[17] All the above and more were planned under Jefferson's leadership with Madison and all the visitors supporting. The school was saturated with nonsectarian religion, and this was done by men who had led the movement for separation of church and state.

And courses in nonsectarian religion are now offered in the university as shown by current catalogues and a personal letter to the author, dated January 24, 1942, from the head of the department, Prof. S. Vernon McCasland.

Jefferson. Jefferson was personally very religious, a Unitarian, but a member, officer, attendant of the Episcopal Church. Before they had a church building in his home town, various sects — Episcopalian, Presbyterian,

Methodist, Baptist—held meetings alternately, with everybody attending, in the court house. Thomas Jefferson attended all and wrote Cooper, "All mix in perfect harmony."[18] When Episcopalians built their church, he drew the plans and supervised the building. He wrote a "wee book" as he called it, *Life and Morals of Jesus of Nazareth,* taken textually from the Gospels, omitting all miracles but including all teaching and parables. It was published forty years ago by the National Congress and is really a very fine work. He wrote John Adams, "An atheist I can never be. I am a Christian."[19] He was a constant and reverent Bible reader. He was liberal with all sects and contributed to the Virginia Bible Society. He died July 4, 1826, and his last words were, "Lord, now lettest thou thy servant depart in peace."[20]

If any man in America knew French secularists and Rousseau and his secular theories of the state and education, as revealed in *Emile,* it was Jefferson, and he plainly turned it down and helped to make this a Christian nation with Christian education as its main bulwark.

Note. Since Jefferson's day, nothing new has been added to modify the principles of religious liberty and separation of church and state. Later provisions against sectarianism were not new. Thomas Jefferson and Horace Mann both understood these principles and used them in their day, putting into education those religious truths common to the sects and excluding controversial teachings. And just that is legal today.

Conclusions

Evidently there is no need to change constitutional provisions. In Jefferson's day they had full right to put religion into the schools free from sectarian taint. We have that right today. What right have we now to demand that it be done? What rights have children, parents, church, citizens?

FUNDAMENTAL PRINCIPLES

PRINCIPAL AUTHORITIES CONSULTED FOR THIS CHAPTER

Arnold, Samuel G., *History of Rhode Island*, Vol. 1, p. 254.

James, Charles F., *Struggle for Religious Liberty in Virginia*. J. B. Bell and Co., 1900.

Foote, *Sketches of Virginia*.

Wells, F. G., *Parish Problems in Virginia*.

Wirt, William, *Life of Patrick Henry*. Lippincott.

Rives, *Life of Madison*.

Williams, John S., *Thomas Jefferson*. Columbia University Press, 1931. *Writings of Jefferson*.

Henning, *Statutes of Virginia*.

Story, Joseph, *The Constitution*.

McAllister, David, *Christian Civil Government*. Sixth Edition, 1927. National Reform Association.

Garner, James W. and Lodge, William C., *History of the United States*. Pub. Howard Severance, 1905.

Congressional Records.

Decisions of United States Supreme Court.

Cabell, Joseph C., *University of Virginia and Letters of Jefferson and Cabell*. Pub. J. W. Randolph, 1856.

Bruce, Phillip A., *History of the University of Virginia*. Macmillan.

Patton, John S., *Jefferson and Cabell and the University of Virginia*. Neale Publishing Co., 1906.

Culberth, David M. R., *The University of Virginia*. Neale Publishing Co., 1908.

Randall, *The Life of Thomas Jefferson*.

Curtis, William A., *Jefferson* and *The True Jefferson*. Lippincott, 1926.

Honeywell, Ray J., *The Educational Work of Thomas Jefferson*. Cambridge University Press, 1941.

REFERENCES TO ABOVE AUTHORS AND WORKS

1. Arnold, Vol. 1, p. 254.
2. *Writings of Jefferson.* Vol. VIII, p. 113.
3. James, p. 170.
4. McAllister, p. 115.
5. Garner and Lodge, Vol. IV, pp. 1584-1588.
6. Wells, p. 56.
7. Cabell, pp. 441 and 474.
8. Patton, pp. 68-74.
9. Curtis, p. 262.
10. Ibid, p. 267.
11. Honeywell, p. 86.
12. Curtis, p. 333.
13. Culberth, p. 117.
14. Bruce, p. 331 and Honeywell, p. 274.
15. Honeywell, p. 111.
16. Curtis, p. 332.
17. Ibid, p. 332.
18. Culbert, pp. 116, 117.
19. Curtis, p. 309.
20. Bruce, p. 21.

VII

RIGHTS OF CHILD, PARENTS, CHURCH, CITIZENS

Rights of the Child

In ancient Greece the child was for the state. At an early age, the boy was taken from parents and trained by the state and for the state. Ancient Sparta boasted, "Our sons are the living walls of Sparta." The boast of democracy is "All for each and each for all." But our modern democracy has swung far to the left. "The state is for the child," at least so in everything but education. In its schools everything is forced upon him except what he needs most— the religious and moral training that will help him to become a good citizen. That alone is denied him. If we want our sons to become the living walls of democracy and not forces for radicalism, irreligion, and crime (which are destroying democracy), we must get back to the former custom described somewhere by Bancroft, our early historian:

"Every child, as it was born into the world, was
lifted from the earth by the ordinances of the land,
and given, at birth, as its birthright, the pledge of
the nation to care for its morals and its mind."

With us, in matters of education, the state
becomes virtually the super-parent, *in loco
parentis.* Whether parents like it or not, the
state forces the child to school six hours a day,
five days a week, nine or more months a year
for ten of the most important years of its life,
and gives the child just such training as the
state wishes, without consulting either parent
or child. If there be any personal liberty left
in our democracy, the child has some inalienable rights that the state must grant—God-
given rights that the state now neglects.

The Children's Charter. In recent years the
government has shown interest in child welfare. In 1909, Theodore Roosevelt called a
conference which resulted in the Children's
Bureau, that has done much for dependent children. In 1919, President Wilson called another,
which dealt with child labor and handicapped
children. In 1929, President Hoover convened
another conference which had to do with child

health and protection. This conference gave us the famous Children's Charter, the first section of which says, *"For every child spiritual and moral training to help him to stand firm under the pressure of life."*[1] The sentence appears almost parenthetical, for its aim seems quite remote from that of the other eighteen sections. Vast good comes to children from these conferences. The question now comes: Why not a conference to promote the "spiritual and moral training" called for by the Children's Charter?

The whole child has a right to be educated. A child is a unit. He is not divisible. He cannot be departmentalized. The whole child goes to school. Education is the symmetrical development of the whole personality. Modern psychology holds that to educate one part of the child and neglect another is to warp the child. The child is not a machine. You cannot make different parts of a child whither and yon and put them together in the assembly room. He is a living organism like a tree, all parts of which must grow together, in constant living touch with each other. And a child has a right to expect that his education shall be conducted after such manner.

The child has a right to be taught correct views of the world and of himself. What is this universe? What am I? Why am I here? What may I become? Every child faces these questions in life. A half truth is a near lie, and may be dangerous. If you teach a child he is the son of an ape and fail to teach him that he may become a child of God, as is done in many schools, he may conclude he is a beast and live like one. Schools must lead pupils of all ages through all the labyrinthian halls of modern science, penetrating to the utmost limit every marvel of this marvelous universe, infinite and infinitesimal, noting always that this is not a "Haeckel's riddle" nor a "Spencer's inscrutable" nor "blind chance," but the handiwork of Him who made us, and with whom we have to do. Children must see this as God's world.

The child has a right to be educated religiously to save himself and the nation from atheism. *The Pittsburgh Press* of October 27, 1929, had a long editorial on "Bringing God Back." It notes a very widely asked question, "Is there a God?" It says the way to overcome the uncertainty is by mass education and points to the schools as the only place it can be done. It suggests an education "which includes religious fundamentals without being in the least degree sectarian." It hints that unless something is done along this line "there may be consequences more disastrous to civilization than the thoughtless suspect," and closes with strong words from Prof. L. P. Jacks, of Cambridge, England, one of the foremost living philosophers:

> "If education goes wrong, what else is like to go right? If the battle of civilization is lost in the schoolroom, who will win it back afterwards? If the whole community is set wrong in its thinking at schools, what chance has the clergy of setting it right from the pulpit? What are the chances of legislation? To begin by starting the community on the wrong road in the plastic period, and then, when it grows up, send out the parson and the policeman to bring it back—what a fool's paradise would compare to that?"

The child has a right to know the proper balance between the material and the spiritual. John Dewey, America's master philosopher, said awhile ago that "external things, the dollar, pleasure, etc., abound too much in

America," unmindful, perhaps, that his own material philosophy helps to sow the seed that brings such harvest. The bread-and-butter theory of education has made that the high purpose of life in America. We must put God back into the schools and teach children that "man cannot live by bread alone," that the supreme task of life is not to make a living but to make a life.

The child has a right to know the Bible as a book. To know the contents of that book is essential to a liberal education: its history and biography; one of the greatest peoples of the human race—the Hebrews; some of the greatest men of all time—Abraham, Moses, David, Isaiah, Paul; the most beautiful poem in all literature, the 23rd Psalm; gripping short stories such as the parables of Jesus, and equally gripping longer stories, concerning Ruth, Esther, Daniel, Joseph; drama, in Job; cogent argument, in Romans; narrative, in the Acts; noble philosophy of life, in the thirteenth chapter of First Corinthians; gems of thought by the hundred. The inspiration of the best in poetry, music, painting, and sculpture is found in the Bible. All modern literature is full of allusions to this book. It is the one source-book, far superior to all others for high ideals of life. Omit the Bible from his education, and the best in the field of culture is lost to the life of your child.

The child has a right to know the Bible and its religion. The Bible is the greatest book in the world, always the world's best seller. Other books guess at the origin of the world and man. The Bible alone tells the story. Without the Bible, history is only kaleidoscopic change, only change. The Bible alone gives the philosophy of history—God working with humans, through humans, to make a better world. Only the Book tells whence we came, why we are here, whither we are going. The Bible alone tells us that we are children of God, brothers to all human beings, workers together with God in making a better world and ourselves becoming fit to live together in a world where dwell righteousness and peace. Only the Bible and its religion reveal the roots of the great social movements of the last 2,000 years in the western world: the emancipation of womanhood; the exaltation of childhood; the birth of freedom and death of slavery; the cry against war; tender regard for the unfortunate; the Ten Commandments which constitute the shortest and completest code of morals the world knows and which is becoming standard for the race. Jesus' law of love and the Golden Rule form the very heart of social ethics, and the thirteenth of First Corinthians is the best social philosophy of life ever penned. Some scientists say we are beasts; the Bible tells us we came from God, belong to God, and may become like Him in character. Pygmy philosophers agree upon nothing except that there is no God; but 3,000 years ago Holy Writ said, "The fool hath said in his heart, there is no God." Rocks beneath and stars above reveal an immutable law controlling all things. Only the Bible reveals God back of and controlling the law. The religion of the Bible is the source of democracy, and only as our children know and live that religion can democracy live and thrive. Liberty bell would lose half its meaning with the Biblical inscription gone. "In God We Trust" is found upon every gold and silver and copper coin of our land. "So help me God" is used at the end of the judicial oath.

Only Bible religion teaches us the meaning and power of these words. Only as American youth know and live the religion of the Bible can they really sing:

> "Our fathers' God, to Thee
> Author of liberty,
> To Thee we sing;
> Long may our land be bright
> With freedom's holy light;
> Protect us by Thy might,
> Great God, our King."

They who leave the Bible and religion out of the training of youth unfit any child—Protestant, Catholic, or Jew—for American citizenship.

Every child has a right to receive character education at school. What is character? *The Christian Statesman* says, "Character is that substance of the soul which determines what a man will do under given circumstances." It is the most vital part of any man. Not what he has, not what he can do, but what he is. It is what makes him a good or bad citizen, an honored member of society or a prison bird. Good character does not just happen. It is a product of education. We have forgotten it so long in our schools that our prisons are crowded and we are the most lawless nation on earth. We neglect character training in schools and force it upon convicts. What folly! What shame!

Every child has a right to be taught morals before he is punished for wrong doing. A very bright fourteen-year-old high school boy, brought before an Iowa court for stealing, admitted the theft but insisted he did not know it was wrong to steal. Investigation revealed that he told the truth. His parents were shiftless, the schools were busy with other matters, and the churches were unable to reach the boy. The wise judge lectured the parents, asked teachers to use the Bible daily, and sentenced the boy to Sunday school. The county clerk told the story in one of our meetings. Many a youth learns and believes, not that it is wrong to steal, but that it is wrong to be caught at it. We send multitudes of boys to prison for crimes we never taught them were crimes—an unpardonable crime against youth. "The right to punish crime involves the duty to teach morality," said Webster.

Every child has a right to be taught the mean-

ing of the Judicial Oath. "In the case now before the court, I promise to tell the truth, the whole truth and nothing but the truth, so help me, God." This is the oath put to every witness in the courtroom. It has been called the bond of society. The religious element gives it its strength. There is a whole system of theology tied up in the four words at the end of the oath, suitable for any theological seminary in the land and as nonsectarian as daylight, admirably suitable also for every schoolroom in the nation. What a simple truth to teach a child! What profound results! Yet, where is the school that teaches it? Very few such schools, if any. Why do they not? Because to do so is thought to be religious and hence taboo. No wonder we have so much perjury in our courts!

If there be any Bill of Rights for children, if there be any regard for our own flesh and blood, every child has an inalienable right to be taught all the above at school. Our democracy, our churches are near the rocks today because we have failed at this point with our children. We must speedily restore God to the public schools, or it is doomsday for our democracy.

Rights of Parents

The state assumes the role of super-parent and takes complete control of every child in the public school system much of the child's time for ten of the most important years of the child's life, and does with the child just what she sees fit without regard to wish of parent or child. The parent must house, feed, clothe, doctor the child; the state requires it, and parents are glad to do that much. But does the right of the parent end there? Is there no Bill of Rights for parents? Has a father no proprietary right in his own flesh and blood?

During the first World War, several states passed laws forbidding the teaching of the German language in public schools. The matter reached Federal Courts, and the highest Court in the land (262 U. S. 404) said that the laws tried improperly to interfere "with the opportunity of pupils to acquire knowledge, not injurious to the health or morals of the child," and German stayed in the schools. In 1922, Oregon passed a law requiring all children within certain age limits to attend public schools. The question went to the high Court, and in 1925 (268 U. S. 510), that body said:

"The child is not merely the creature of the
state; those who nurture him and direct his destiny have the right coupled with the high duty,
to recognize and prepare him for additional
duties."

And the parochial school lives today.

But a short while since a public educational
institution in New York contracted with Bertrand Russell to teach in their school. A mother
asked the court to set aside the contract on the
ground that Russell's teaching would corrupt
the morals of her daughter. After examining
Russell's writings, the court set aside the contract. A cry went up from some teachers for
an appeal on the ground of academic freedom,
but no appeal was taken. None will be taken,
for every thoughtful man knows that schools
are not made for teachers and half-baked
theories and dangerous doctrines and personal
vagaries of teachers, but for boys and girls, the
men and women of tomorrow, to make them
keen of intellect and clean of character, safe
citizens of the nation.

So there is a Bill of Rights for parents. No
question but that a vast multitude of parents
agree with P. P. Claxton, ex-Commissioner of

Education of the United States, who said, "I want my child taught religion at school."[2] Only a small minority oppose God in the schoolhouse, and now only these seem to have any bill of rights.

It would improve matters greatly if parents in any community would go to the school board and demand a bit of academic freedom for their own teachers, not to teach the risque, salacious, off-color, but to give the children some of those great religious and moral truths that are the essential foundation of good character and good citizenship. Multitudes of teachers would gladly do so if they felt they had the backing of parents.

Rights of the Church, or Churches

When the fathers separated church and state and built the public school system, it was not their aim to antagonize the churches nor hurt religion. Nor is such the effort of the schools today, but in effect it amounts to that. The schools are not satisfied with six hours a day of the child's time, but so crowd him with home work that he has little time or energy left for religion and the church. This is often true when children are in the grades, but it is notoriously so in high school. All over the nation, the cry goes up that high school students are noticeably absent from church, and necessary home work is the student's excuse. Many of these students, absent from church during high school days, become permanently estranged from the church.

That is not all, nor the worst. If the religious note were effectively sounded in the schools, there would be some compensation to children for the loss of time from the churches. But with God shut out of the schools, as is the widespread practice today, the effect (as abundantly shown by the thoughtful discerning men quoted in the first chapter) is "to leave the schools *not neutral,* but to exert an influence *against* religion," to put the schools under "pagan" control, to suggest to youth that "religion is of minor importance if it has any value," with the result to multitudes of youth that "religious indifference becomes their creed." All this is resulting "in the steady decline of religion and the steady growth of secularism, another name for atheism," leading to a situation "fraught with danger," imperiling "the future of religion," even "the life of the nation," indeed "the very life of our civilization" through "irreligion and crime."

Nor is this all. When the foundations of the nation shake through crime, when churches face appalling religious indifference and secularism, when ministers and church leaders battle with back against the wall, scarcely able to hold their own, it is widely charged that they are the ones at fault, that they lie down on the job, that if they did their duty conditions would be all right.

It seems high time for church leaders to assert themselves and demand in every corner of the land, in every church, in every parent-teacher's meeting, in every school board, in every legislature, that churches have right to some of the time of the children after school hours, that God must be restored to the schools of the land as He used to be, and that the churches be given what Lynn Harold Hough called "a noble sort of fair play."[3] This is not only the right of every churchman, but it is his duty as a citizen.

Rights of Citizens

Who? You and I and all the rest of us—that

unorganized, heterogenous, inarticulate, help-
less mass of humanity living in every corner of
the land, in daily danger of the thief, robber,
rapist, murderer, with no protection but a cry,
stifled perhaps in the giving; every possible
martyr of the merciless murderer; every man
who may look down the muzzle of the gun of
the hold-up man; every victim of the purse-
snatcher; every man whose car may be stolen,
or who pays higher insurance against theft of
his car; every wife, mother, sister, daughter,
prospective victim of the rapist, who must submit or die, or both; every man whose bank
account is endangered by the hold-up man or
the embezzler; and so on ad infinitum.

The taxpayer, what of him specifically? A
system bad for morals cannot be good eco-
nomics. We are told that crime costs us fifteen
billion dollars a year. That means $120.00 for
every man, woman and child in the nation.
Bibles in the hands of schoolteachers would
be far more effective to reduce crime than
policemen's clubs, criminal courts, and prison
cells, and infinitely more humane. A Michigan
banker said, "I am not interested in the Bible

in the schools," and got the answer: "Bibles in the hands of schoolteachers would be far better protection to your bank than that sign in your window—'$1,000 reward for the capture, dead or alive, of any man who robs this bank.'" A recent letter from the W. A. Alexander Insurance Company of Chicago says that burglary and hold-up insurance rates are 20 per cent less in New York City, Philadelphia, Washington, Baltimore, and Pittsburgh than in Cleveland, Detroit, Chicago, St. Louis, and Los Angeles. Incidentally the Book is in daily use in the schools of the first five cities and carefully shut out of the schools of the last five. It would be good economics to return religion to the schools, for the saving in the crime bill would soon pay all expenses of our public school system.

REFERENCES

1. *White House Conference Reports*, D. Appleton and Co., New York.
2. *World's Moral Problems*, National Reform Association, p. 313.
3. *Religious Education Journal*, June, 1927, p. 586.

VIII

STATUTES, DECISIONS, CUSTOMS

Present Bible Reading in Schools

The Bible is now read devotionally every day in the public schools of about forty million Americans, nearly a third of our entire population—mainly a quite recent return to the old custom. Twelve states by mandatory law read a portion of Scripture every day in every schoolroom. The states, with the dates of the passage of the law, are as follows: Massachusetts, 1855; Pennsylvania, 1913; Tennessee, 1915; New Jersey, 1916; Alabama, 1919; Georgia, 1921; Maine and Delaware, 1923; Kentucky, 1924; Florida and Idaho, 1925; Arkansas, 1930. Many large cities outside these states, headed by New York City, Baltimore, Washington, D. C., by school board rule, use the Bible devotionally every day in all schoolrooms. Our latest investigation about three years ago revealed thirty-eight cities of over 100,000 population (almost half of such cities in the nation) use the Bible with religious intent daily in all rooms. Besides, the Book is read daily in the schools of hundreds of smaller towns and cities and villages and rural sections all over the land. This great change for the better came very largely during the fifteen years just before 1930. Since then, during the depression, the bread-and-butter problem has been so much to the fore that other matters have been forgotten.

In addition to the above twelve states, eight others by law forbid the exclusion of the Bible from their schools—Iowa, Indiana, the two Dakotas, Kansas, Oklahoma, Mississippi, New York, the latter applying to the metropolis only. Thus, twenty states by definite law require the daily use of the Bible in their schools or specifically forbid its exclusion therefrom.

Six other states have decisions from their highest courts giving the Book complete right of way in the public schools: Ohio, Michigan, Minnesota, Nebraska, Colorado, and Texas. According to this count, so far there are twenty-six states that either by definite statute or supreme court decision open schoolhouse doors to the Book of God. The Supreme Courts of Illinois and Washington shut schoolhouse doors against the Bible. The high Courts of Wisconsin and Louisiana give split decisions, partly closing the doors to the Book. The South Dakota Court argues against the Bible in the schools but leaves it there. There is considerable uncertainty, but it seems that by interpretation, attorneys general or state superintendents exclude the Bible from the schools of six states: California, Nevada, Arizona, Wyoming, Utah, and upstate New York. We find no law, court decision, or official interpretation that interferes with the use of the Bible in the schools of the remaining eleven states: Vermont, New Hampshire, Connecticut, Rhode Island, Maryland, Virginia, West Virginia, North Carolina, South Carolina, Missouri, and Oregon. In some of these states, correspondence shows the Bible in large use in the schools; in others little attention is given to the religious note.

State Supreme Court Decisions

The supreme courts of eighteen states have faced the question of the right of the Bible in their schools, one of them, Iowa, twice. The states with the citation and date of decision are as follows: Maine, 38 Me. 379 (1855); Massachusetts, 12 Allen 127 (1866); Ohio, 23 Ohio 211 (1872); Iowa, 64 Ia. 367 (1884); Wisconsin, 76 Wis. 177 (1890); Michigan, 119 Mich. 560 (1898); Nebraska, 65 Neb. 853 (1902); Kansas, 69 Kan. 53 (1904); Kentucky, 120 Ky. 608 (1905); Texas, 104 Texas 1 (1908); Illinois, 245 Ill. 334 (1910); Louisiana, 136 La. 1034 (1915); Washington, 102 Wash. 369 (1918); Iowa, 182 Ia. 691 (1918); Georgia, 152 Ga. (1821); California, 193 Calif. 54 (1924); Colorado, 81 Colo. 276 (1927); Minnesota, 171 Minn. 142 (1927); S. Dakota, 226-2 N. W. 348 (1929).

The Washington and second Iowa cases dealt with other matters and touched Bible reading only incidentally. The California decision considered only the right of the Bible in school libraries as a reference book, and was satisfactory in that it held the Bible not sectarian either in King James or Douay versions. All other cases dealt directly and solely with Bible reading in the schools. In Washington and Louisiana the decisions turned on peculiar statements in their state constitutions. In all other states the constitutions are virtually alike on matters involved.

In all these eighteen cases, every phase of every objection to the right of the Bible in the schools was presented by the very best attorneys money could employ, and in spite of that fact there have been surprisingly favorable decisions from the courts. We Americans have magnified the rights of the individual to the *n*th degree and reduced the rights of the people almost to the vanishing point. This has hurt us tremendously both in the courts and schools, and in our national life. But the *principles have not changed, and the courts, when the facts were properly presented, have sustained the principles with surprising unanimity.* In the sixteen states whose constitutions are virtually alike on the matters involved, thirteen supreme courts threw the doors of schoolhouses wide open to the Book of God, and in two of the other three, there is good evidence that the courts did not have all the facts in hand. It would require a volume to discuss the decisions adequately, but some facts can and must be presented.

General Conclusions

The courts generally agree that religion in the schools is on the same plane as religious services in legislatures, army, navy, prisons, etc.; that such services do not transform the schoolhouse into a place of worship, do not diminish civil rights, do not force religion upon anybody, but merely give rights to those who wish them without imposing upon anyone. They agree that the Bible is not sectarian. They also agree that objection of a child or sect to its use is "unreasonable" and would lead to "absurd and hurtful conclusions," would put the "schools under control of children" or a "sect," and "would produce conditions bordering on moral anarchy." The Michigan and Colorado Courts held that a man is "intolerant" to object to the reading of the Bible in school when his own child is not required to be present.

On Separation of Church and State

Separation of church and state is the objection presented most frequently by speakers opposing religion in public education. But lawyers know better, and have presented this objection but once before a high court—in the

Georgia case. According to the Georgia Court, the Federal Constitution has nothing to do with the subject of the Bible in public education. Concerning the objection, the Court said, "It should be distinctly understood that this is not a movement of separation of the state from Christianity." The Court showed at considerable length that separation of church and state does not mean excluding religion from national life. *The courts of this country, from the Federal Supreme Court down, insist that this is in no sense a secular nation.*

On Religious Liberty

The South Dakota case gives an unfortunate view of this principle of religious liberty. Under the school board rule, children might be excused, if they so desired, during the Bible reading. But in their going they made so much confusion that the board changed the rule and required all to be present, though none need take part in the exercises. On advice of parents some children refused to remain and were expelled, but could return on pledge of obedience. They sued for reinstatement without pledge, and by three-to-two vote, the court

149

ordered reinstatement. The majority said:

> "It is essential to religious liberty that one be free to worship according to the dictates of his own conscience, and not only that, but to live and teach his religion. That right cannot be taken away by the state, and it follows that such teachings belong exclusively to individuals and voluntary organizations. The state as an educator must keep out of this field. The parent's liberty of conscience is the controlling factor and not that of the child."—226 2 N. W. 354.

The statement denies liberty *to* worship and permits only liberty *not* to worship, and amounts to tyranny. The logic is fatally faulty, as will be seen later.

In a similar situation, the Kansas Court held that a child exercised his religious liberty by listening or letting his mind wander where it would during the reading. The Massachusetts Court held that no right of the child is violated when he is required to be present, so long as he is not required to take part. The Texas Court said:

> "It does not follow that one or more individuals have the right to have the courts deny the people the privilege of having their children instructed in the moral truths of the Bible because such objec-

tors do not desire that their own children shall be participants therein. This would be to starve the moral and spiritual natures of the many out of deference of the few."—104 Texas 1.

In the Michigan case a father refused to ask that his son be excused and tried to shut the Bible out of the schoolroom. The Court said:

"Does it harm one who does not care for conscientious reasons to listen to readings from the Bible, that others are given the opportunity to do so? Is it not intolerant for one not required to attend to object to such reading?"—109 Mich. 560.

In Maine the Bible was used as a school reader, and a father wanted it excluded because to read it would violate the conscience of his daughter and the order of his church. As to the child the Court said:

"As the existence of conscientious scruples to the reading of a book can only be known, from the assertions of the child, its mere assertion must suffice for the exclusion of any book in the reading or hearing of which it may allege a wrong to be done to its religious conscience. The claim, so far as it rests upon conscience, is a claim to annul any regulation of the state made by its constituted authorities. As a right existing on the part of one

151

child, it is equally a right belonging to all. As it relates to one book, so it may relate to another, whether relating to conscience or morals. As the child may object to the reading of any book, it may object to hearing it read, for the same cause—and thus the power of selection of books is withdrawn from those to whom the law entrusts it, and by right of negation is transferred to the scholars. The right, as claimed, undermines the power of the state. It is that the will of the majority shall bow to the conscience of the minority, or of one. Nor is this all. While the laws are made for those of full age, the right of obstruction, of interdiction, is given to any and all children, of however immature age or judgment."—38 Me. 379.

As to the objection raised by the father that the rules violated the order of his church, the Court said:

"If the Bible, or any version of it, may be excluded from the schools, because its reading may be opposed to the teaching of the authorities of any church, the same result may ensue to any other book. If one sect may object, the same right must be granted to others. This would give the authorities of any sect the right to annual any regulation of the constituted authorities of the state, as to course of study and books used. It is placing the education of the state at once and forever, in subordination to the decrees and teachings of any

and all sects, when their members conscientiously
believe such teachings. It at once surrenders the
power of a state to a government not emanating
from the people nor recognized by the constitution."—38 Me. 379.

The Court also said:

"Salus populi suprema lex est (the welfare of the
people is the supreme law) is a maxim of universal
application; and when liberty of conscience would
interfere with the paramount rights of the public,
it must be restrained."—38 Me. 379.

This last phase of liberty is little thought of
these days by those who oppose religion in the
schools. In their warped thinking, individuals
have all the rights and the state is bound hand
and foot. Where else do we have such lati-
tudinarian construction of liberty of conscience? Do we burn our schoolhouses because
some believe that ignorance is bliss? Do we
refrain from hanging murderers because the
practice hurts tender consciences? The Maine
Court held that the people as a whole have some
rights that individuals must respect. The South
Dakota Court did not consider any of the above
decisions except that of Maine, and when it
could not get around the words of that Court,

called it "a far-fetched excuse." The South Dakota Court held that all the people must bow to a few. No other court agrees with its contention.

The Colorado Court gives a far better decision on a very similar set of facts. It held that the Bible has a right in the schools, and that the children might be absent during the exercises if they chose. South Dakota makes much of liberty of conscience, and swings the case on that principle, but it nowhere defines the principle, and actually seems to misunderstand its meaning. Its ruling brings tyranny, not liberty, while the Colorado ruling brings liberty, not tyranny. The Colorado case was decided two years before that of Dakota, and just why the latter Court failed to cite a decision so recent in a neighboring state is a bit surprising.

The King James Version

Catholics hold that the King James Version of the Bible is sectarian, and Illinois and South Dakota Courts agree with that view, the former with no argument. The high courts of Maine, Kentucky, Iowa, Minnesota, Nebraska, Colorado, Georgia, California and the Federal Supreme Court hold it not sectarian. The

Kentucky Court gives a fine discussion of the subject, as follows:

"That the Bible, or any particular version of it has been adopted by one denomination as authentic, or by them asserted to be inspired, cannot make it a sectarian book. The book itself to be sectarian, must show that it teaches the particular dogmas of a sect as such, and not alone that it is so comprehensive as to include them by the partial interpretation of its adherents. Nor is a book sectarian because it is edited or compiled by those of a particular sect. It is not the authorship, nor the mechanical composition of the book, nor its use, but its contents that determine its character. If the legislature or the constitutional convention had intended that the Bible should be proscribed, they would have said so. The word 'Bible' is shorter and better understood than the word 'sectarian.' It is not conceivable that, if they had intended to exclude the Bible from the public schools, this purpose would be obscured within a controversial word."—120 Ky. 608.

The California Court adds a good word:

"The statute makes the character of a book the test of whether it is 'sectarian,' not the authorship or extent of its approval by different sects or by all. The fact that the King James version of the Bible is commonly used by the Protestant Church and not by Catholics does not make its character sectarian; its character is what it is, a widely accepted version of the Bible, and this is equally applicable to the Douay version, neither being a book of sectarian character within the meaning of the statute."

The Supreme Court of the United States held that the King James version is not sectarian. Stephen Girard left a large sum of money to build and sustain a home and school for orphan boys and ordered that sectarian matters be excluded. In 1844, a case came before the high Court seeking to break the will on the ground that it violated the Christian principles of the land. In the opinion (2 Howard U. S. 200), the court discriminated between "sectarians and sectarianism" on the one hand and Christian instructors and Bible teaching on the other. It said in part:

"All that can be gathered from his language is that he desired to exclude sectarians and sectarianism from the college, leaving the instructors and officers free to teach the purest morality, the love of truth, sobriety and industry, by all appropriate means, and of course including the best, the surest and most impressive. Why may not the Bible, and especially the New Testament, without

156

note or comment, be read and taught, as a divine
revelation, in the college—its general principles
expounded, its evidences explained, and its glori-
ous principles of morality inculcated?"

The Court used the above words as the hinge
upon which the case swung. They permitted the
use of the Bible in the school in face of the
fact that "sectarians and sectarianism" are
excluded by the terms of the will. In using the
words "without note or comment," the Court
seems to suggest *what* version to use while the
words "taught, expounded, explained, inculcated" tell *how* it may be used, much the same
as in the New York law mentioned in Chapter
III.

*Also in these days when so many insist that
the Bible and religion cannot be used in the
schools without sectarianism, it is worth while
to note that the Court of last resort clearly held
that the Bible may "be read and taught,
expounded, explained, inculcated," all without sectarian taint.*

The South Dakota Court compared the King
James and Douay versions, found a few differences and without calling the former sectarian,
held it improper for school use. Let us suggest a

better way: *When a man attacks any version as sectarian, require him to show in court some teaching of that version that his church denies, or some teaching of his church that the version denies.* This would stop all caviling.

But why all this fuss about versions? They are so nearly alike that only an expert can tell the difference. Some, like the South Dakota Court, would burn the ship to kill a few rats. *While we strain out the gnat of sectarianism and swallow the camel of secularism in education, we prepare a poison potion that will kill the nation.* While we fuss, the devil is gloatingly getting America. In mixed schools, why not have on the teacher's desk for school use several versions, including the Douay version?

It is encouraging to note that the Catholic version of the New Testament recently off the press does not contain, so far as we can find, the controversial words used in their former version. The word "daily" now takes the place of "super-substantial" in the Lord's Prayer, and the word "repent" is now used instead of "do penance" in several places. These changes should go far to make either version satisfactory to both groups.

Some Particular Court Decisions

The Washington decision, completely excluding the Bible from its schools, and the decision of Louisiana, faintly hinting dropping the New Testament, stand upon peculiarities in their state constitutions and need no discussion here.

The Wisconsin and Nebraska decisions are often misconstrued. The former forbade the indiscriminate use of the Bible in the schools, but did say that certain portions might and should be used. It said:

> "To teach of a supreme being of infinite wisdom, power and goodness, and that it is the highest duty of all men to adore, love and obey Him is not sectarian. There is much in the Bible that cannot be characterized as sectarian. . . . It may be used to inculcate good morals. . . . No more complete code of morals exists than is contained in the New Testament."—76 Wis. 177.

The original Nebraska decision seemed to exclude the Bible from education in the state. But on request for a rehearing, the chief justice so interpreted the decision as to completely reverse its effect and intent. He said "the law does not forbid the use of the Bible in either version in the schools."—65 Neb. 853.

The Ohio decision, from its priority in point of time and some striking language by the court, comments by the way (*obiter dicta,* as the lawyers say), has been most devastatingly used over the nation for many years. But the decision did not close the schoolrooms to the Book that made our civilization. The court did say that the law left the whole matter in the hands of the school boards to put the Bible in or out of the schools.—23 Ohio 211.

The Illinois decision (245 Ill. 334) can scarcely be considered dispassionately. It looks like collusion between the lawyers and muddled thinking by the court. No evidence was presented in any court, as the lawyers agreed on the facts. They agreed that children were required to be present and join in the worship, which was not true, and the court made this false presentment the basis for holding that Bible reading in the schools violates religious liberty. Purely on its own *ipse dixit,* with no argument or evidence to support it, the court held the King James version and reading from it, sectarian instruction, prohibited by the state constitution. As a side light, it is interesting to know that the provision of the state constitution on which the court relied to call the King James version sectarian was sent to the constitutional convention forty years before by a large body of Methodist ministers, with the request that it be embodied in the constitution then being prepared. It was adopted by the convention with minor changes and used by the court to shut the Bible out of the schools forty years later. Perhaps those preachers did not dream how courts could twist language and make it mean what it was not intended to mean.

In this case appellant counsel argued at great length that the constitutional convention intended to shut the Bible out of the schools and misquoted speeches made in the convention to suit his purpose. Defense counsel answered this point very briefly, in a single paragraph, and utterly ignored a vast array of facts that would have completely disproved the charge against the convention. Long after the sections of the constitution relied on by the court to exclude the Bible from the schools had been adopted by the convention, a resolution came in to add a specific provision forbidding the exclusion of the Book from the schools. It was debated a whole day. Every word was taken down stenographically and printed and is now available in the Chicago and other public libraries. One man spoke against the Bible in education. Seventeen men held that the Bible has a right in the schools. The proposal was side-stepped because of general agreement that there was no need of it, that the Bible was then in the schools and would remain there with no specific word in the constitution—a conclusion that proved a fatal blunder.[1]

Very able dissenting opinion was given by two judges who charged that the majority completely reversed all previous rulings of the court on similar matters and that they had quoted no authority to sustain their position and that none could be found. But the ruling stands, and the Bible is out of Illinois schools today.

The South Dakota decision needs a further word. There is plain evidence of muddled thinking by the court. They twisted facts about other court decisions. Their minds seemed closed beforehand to the issues before them. They ignored the rule of practical construction that long unquestioned use is presumption of right— ignored the fact that since 1883 the law had named the Bible as of right in the schools. But space will not permit further discussion here. It was a three-to-two decision with a strong dissenting opinion by the two.

The Kansas Court gave a very fine statement of the function of the schools and of the place of the Bible therein, as follows:

"Every pupil who enters the public schools has a right to expect, and the public has a right to demand of the teacher, that each pupil shall come out with a more acute sense of right and wrong, higher ideals of life, a more independent and manly character, a higher conception of his duty as a citizen, and a more laudable ambition in life than when he entered. The system ought to be so maintained as to make this certain. The noblest ideals of character are found in the Bible. To emulate these is the supreme conception of citizenship. It could not, therefore, have been the intention of the framers of our constitution to impose the duty upon the legislature of establishing a system of common schools where morals are to be inculcated and exclude therefrom the lives of the persons who possessed the highest moral attainments."—69 Kan. 53.

The Texas Court saw clearly and spoke well. After putting religion in the schools on the same plane with such services in all other state institutions (legislature, asylums, prisons, etc.) the court added:

"To hold that the offering of prayer and singing of hymns and reading the Bible makes the place where it is done a place of worship would produce intolerable results.... Christianity is so interwoven with the web and woof of the state government that to sustain such a contention that the state constituition prohibits the reading of the Bible, offering prayer or singing hymns of a religious character in any public school building would produce a condition bordering on moral anarchy. The absurd and hurtful consequences furnish a strong argument against the soundness of the contention. . . . It does not follow that one or more individuals have the right to have the courts deny the people the privilege of having their children instructed in the moral truths of the Bible because such objectors did not desire that their own children be participants therein. This would be to starve the moral nature of the many out of deference to the few."— 104 Texas 1.

The Colorado Court broke new ground when it said:

> "The state for her own protection may require the children to be educated . . . certain studies plainly essential to good citizenship must be taught . . . .unquestionably much in the Bible is plainly essential to good citizenship."—81 Colo. 276.

Two of the judges even went so far as to say, "that the Book is so essential to good citizenship that parents may not exclude it from the instruction of their children." The case also reached new and higher ground when the Fourteenth Amendment to the Federal Constitution was brought in. The opinion notes (262 U. S. 390), that the Federal High Court said that "states may not shut out of the schools what is not injurious to the health, morals or beyond the understanding of an ordinary child." From these words, friends of religion in public education have high hopes that when a case reaches the Federal Court on a proper basis, as it will, all controversy will end, and thenceforth religion will have a recognized, rightful place in our educational system.

So far, we have found that religion in the schools violates no fundamental principle of our government, that Bible reading in school is generally legal, even widely practiced, and is becoming increasingly required. Before proceeding further with the main argument, it seems necessary to consider more at length the meaning of the words, sect and sectarian.

REFERENCE

1. *Proceedings Illinois Constitutional Convention*, 1870, pp. 1739-1761.

IX

SECT AND SECTARIAN

In the light of previous discussion, it would seem that this subject of sect and sectarian need not be considered. But it has come to the fore in modern days, and is now vital. Upon the meaning our laws give to these two words hangs finally the right of the Bible in the schools, especially the New Testament. Two questions are involved.

1. Do the adjectives, religious and sectarian, mean the same? Samuel Windsor Brown in his *"Secularization of American Education"* assumes that they do and that twenty-nine states thereby exclude the Bible from their schools. And he has a wide following. But is he right?

The word, sect, and its derivatives have been in our language and laws much over a century. In 1827, Massachusetts forbade the use of public school funds to purchase books "calculated to

favor any particular religious sect or tenet."
In seeking to enforce this law, on June 23, 1838,
Horace Mann wrote, "Such vast good may be
accomplished by a union of effort on points on
which we agree that it seems little better than
suicidal perpetually to fasten attention upon
those wherein we differ."[1] On July 23, 1838, he
wrote: "The points of doctrine on which good
and great men differ shall not be obtruded into
the mutual grounds of the schools."[2] "The
religion of heaven shall be taught to the children while the creeds of men shall be post-
poned."[3] The rule of the State Board of Education on September 1, 1838, "enjoins that children *shall* be taught the principles common to
all the sects and thus wisely leaves to parents
and the several denominations to complete the
system each according to his own views."[4] In
1818, the Jefferson report to the Virginia Legislature (Chap. VI) said that "the proofs of the
Being of God, the creator, preserver and ruler
of the universe" may be taught and that "every
sect provide further instruction in their own
particular tenets." The Supreme Court of
Wisconsin said: "To teach of a supreme being
of infinite wisdom power and goodness, etc.

[evidently religious], is not sectarian" (Chapter VIII).

In the discussion of this subject the Supreme Court of Colorado said:

"Sectarian means pertaining to a sect, and when put into the Constitution in 1875-76, was commonly used to describe things pertaining to the various sects of Christianity, and was not extended beyond the various religious sects. A sectarian doctrine or tenet, then, would be one peculiar to one or more of these sects, as, for example, the doctrine held by Baptists that immersion is necessary to valid baptism, a practice which many other sects tolerate but do not require. This was the view taken by the Supreme Court of the United States in the Girard Will Case."

Continuing the Court said:

"If all religious instruction were prohibited no history could be taught. . . . Nearly all the histories of New England and indeed of the United States are bound up with religion, religious inferences, implications and other prejudices. . . . Further if we are to take the argument of the plaintiff that sectarian means more than the sects of religion and say that it means religious, we must push it to its logical limit, and say that believers are a sect, and that, in deference to atheists, no reference to

169

God may be made and this would bar the singing
of "America" and the "'Star Spangled Banner";
and, if we would say that sectarian means religious,
we would bar not only the greatest of our poets,
including Shakespeare and Milton whose inspir-
ing messages have a religious basis, but the greatest of our orators, Webster, Clay and Lincoln." . . .
"Religious and sectarian are not synonymous."—
81 Colo. 276.

In the Girard Will Case (Chapter VIII)
the Supreme Court of the United States said:
"Why may not the Bible, especially the New
Testament, be read and taught . . . expounded
. . . inculcated," while sectarianism is excluded?
To the above may be added the laws of many
states requiring or permitting the Bible (i.e.
a religious book) while sectarian matters are
specifically shut out.

All the above reveals a positive difference
between the two words. *Religious doctrines
are those on which the Christian sects agree.
Sectarian doctrines are those on which Christian sects do not agree.* The laws of New York,
Kansas, and Oklahoma on the subject of the
Bible in the schools use both words, but the
language seems redundant, for the law specifically permits the Book in the schools.

2. **Are Jews a sect within American law?**
If so, the New Testament has no right in our
schools, for our laws admit to the schools only
those doctrines on which Christian sects agree.
The question here is, Are the words sect and
religion synonymous? The Standard Diction-
ary mentions "the various sects of Jews,
Mohammedans or Christians" and indicates
that the word sect includes different groups
within a religion. Sadducees and Pharisees
were sects among the Jews. Catholics, Presbyterians, Baptists are sects among Christians.
This is the meaning of our laws on the subject
as well as the usage of our language and of
language generally. This is the only construction that can be put upon the laws of many
states and decisions of many courts that give
the Bible (both Old and New Testaments) right
of way in our schools. This is in harmony with
the tacit admission of the Federal Supreme
Court in the Girard Will Case and their plain
declaration in the Trinity Church Case that
"THIS IS A CHRISTIAN NATION."

When the Ohio Supreme Court went out of
its way in the Cincinnati case and said: "Legal
Christianity is a solecism"; when the Illinois

Supreme Court said: "The Bible is a sectarian book to the Jew," they both, with no argument, went counter to the whole history of this nation and the twice-repeated declaration of the highest Court in the land as well as the laws and court decisions of many states.

Thus Jews and Christians are not different sects, for Judaism and Christianity are different religions. In fact no Jew would be willing to admit that he belonged to a sect of Christians. Thus no Jew can come into court and ask that the New Testament be excluded from the schools on the ground that it is sectarian.

I am not attacking the Jews. I merely quote the law of the land, made by the fathers a century and a half ago. Nor is the law an attack upon the Jews. Our nation builders had nothing against the Jew. They gave him perfect religious liberty. He has it today. But those nation builders chose to make this nation Christian, and they set up, as one of the vital bulwarks of the nation, the right to use the New Testament in the schools. And the evidence is close at hand that the construction of the action of the fathers as noted here is correct, Jews being judges. New York City probably has a larger Jewish population than any other city in the world, and the New Testament has been used in the schools of the city much more than a century. But no Jew has ever gone to court and asked that it be excluded on sectarian grounds. If any Jew of today believes the construction herein is incorrect, he has a perfect right to bring a test case into the courts of the Empire State, or of almost any other state.

Three words may be said to the Jews, all kindly.

When the Old Testament is in the schools, the Jewish religion is there, for the Jewish *Holy Scriptures* in English, except in two brief statements, resemble very closely the Protestant versions, and these differences would probably never be mentioned in school. And when that Jewish boy is taught the great religious and moral truths of his own religion at school, he will later face the world much better prepared to live than if he had none of such teaching, as multitudes of Jewish and Gentile children now face it. Even if he does get at school a little of the New Testament that he does not accept, he is not compelled to believe it.

Christian Americans think the Jew the most

persecuted race the world has known and do not sympathize with the persecutors. And we think that the message of Christ in our public schools is the only influence that in the years to be will keep this land a safe place for the Jew, where he can live in peace and enjoy his own religion. We think, too, that the Jew should see this for himself and gladly join to keep this land a safe place of refuge for him and his by at least not opposing Christianity in our schools.

There is much to be done before every child in this land can have at school (the only place multitudes can ever get it) the message of morals and religion that will make him a safe citizen in the days ahead. Much of that message is believed by both Jew and Gentile, Catholic and Protestant. There is no good reason why Christian and Jew cannot co-operate a long way in putting that message into our schools. Of course to make this land safe for the Jew tomorrow, we must not denature the Christian message. But there is much in which all can co-operate and thus make it better for us all.

SECT AND SECTARIAN

REFERENCES

1. Culver, Raymond B., *Horace Mann and Religion in Massachusettts Public Schools*, by Yale University Press, 1929, p. 62.
2. Ibid., p. 73.
3. Ibid., p. 76.
4. Ibid., p. 48.

X

CHRISTIAN PUBLIC EDUCATION LEGAL

Christian public education is legal in most states but not in all. No law calls the Bible sectarian. No state law excludes it by name from any school. By doubtful construction of one word in her constitution, Louisiana shuts out the New Testament. Illinois and South Dakota decisions excluding the Bible are denied by other courts and will not stand close inspection. Washington, Utah, and Arizona's constitutions, phrased alike, appear to exclude religion from the schools. The Idaho constitution forbids "sectarian and religious doctrines." Oklahoma forbids "sectarian or religious doctrines," but specifically permits "reading of the Holy Scriptures." With these exceptions, no law plainly forbids Christian teaching. In fact it needs no extended argument to prove Christian public education legal now. Indeed in this Christian nation, if religion be in the schools at all, common sense would say it must be Christian.

By Christian public education we mean teaching in the public schools by suitable teachers employed by the state as a regular part of the curriculum, the great moral and religious truths of the Bible with special emphasis upon the teachings of Jesus. The ethical parts must be prominent, but there must be enough of the truths of religion generally accepted by our people to give binding force to the moral obligations. Let the supreme authority of Jesus in matters of religion and conduct be assumed. Dogmatic assertions about His person or nature would be out of place. The course should be mandatory in all elementary and secondary grades. Sectarianism must be absent. By suitable teachers, we mean those found by the state to be willing, competent and of good character, teaching by word and deed, regardless of denominational affiliations. The real aim of it all must be good citizenship, not to bolster the churches but to save the state.

Special Mention

Idaho. Note the folly of Idaho's legal inhibition. The State Board of Education, feeling the injury of her law to the children, got the legislature to require daily Bible reading in all schools under the subterfuge of "character building and literary values" and then injected such passages as the first and the twenty-third Psalms under the title of "Great Songs and Lyrics." Must teachers bootleg religion into the schools by tricking legislators? Better boot the foolish words out of the constitution.

Attorneys General always lean to the objector. In California the attorney general opposed the Bible in the schools on sectarian grounds, but in 1924, the State Supreme Court held the Book not sectarian. Then he opposed it on religious grounds though nothing in the law forbids religion in the schools. Wyoming is in the same boat with even less reason. And Michigan, too, though the whole history and practice of the state, even a State Supreme Court decision, deny the contention. But the opinions bind nobody and are often upset by supreme courts.

Delaware and New Jersey laws require daily Bible reading and permit the Lord's Prayer by name and say other than this "no religious service or exercise." However, they omit the word, instruction, and naught but a strained construction would forbid religious instruction in class.

Upstate New York. For much over a century the state head of the schools has ruled out Bible reading not on legal but on purely prudential grounds, and has even tried to make it appear that the constitutional convention of 1894 intended to exclude the Bible from the schools, though that body definitely said they did not so intend.

"Without comment." These words occur in the laws of five states that require daily Bible reading in all schools, and are generally believed to exclude all other religion. We think the belief groundless. The restriction applies during opening exercises, and the law is silent about religious instruction at other times. If the legislature had intended to exclude such teaching at other times, it chose a very far-fetched and unfortunate way of saying so. They could very easily have put the prohibition in far plainer and simpler words, free from possible misconstruction. The absence of plain restriction is strong presumption that none was intended. And history supports the presumption. In years bygone there was much religion in the schools, but later without sanction of law it was crowded out by aggressive minorities and by the indifference of the majorities. At least, in Massachusetts, Pennsylvania, New Jersey and, we believe, in Tennessee, patriotic organizations asked the legislature to pass the law in question, and it seems to us very unreasonable for them to sponsor a bill saying *only that much* when their plain intent was *at least that much*. Their effort was to hold the Bible in the schools, not partly to shut it out. Again, at least thirty states have no such legal restriction, and the laws of seven states require the daily use of the Book with no such restriction. Shall Massachusetts and Pennsylvania, always in the past among the foremost states in holding God in the schools, now, by a needless construction, join the most backward states in almost shutting the schoolroom door in His face? Will the Christian teachers of Pennsylvania, "a Christian state," to use the word of her own Supreme Court, join in ushering Christ almost out of the schools, or in turning Him the cold shoulder, if not quite permitted to exclude Him, and do it by doubtful interpretation of the law? We do not think so.

The title of the Pennsylvania Bible-Reading law very plainly shows that it was not the intent of the law to forbid religious instruction, but merely to hold the instruction during opening exercises within certain limits. The title says: "An Act regulating the reading of the Holy Bible . . . . Whereas the rules and regulations governing the reading of the Holy Bible in the public schools of this Commonwealth are not uniform," etc.

Strictly Legal Phases

Except in the five states above named, it seems to us perfectly legal to give Christian instruction in public schools for the following reasons, in addition to what has already been said:

Silence gives consent. The laws of at least twenty states make no mention of religion in the schools, and it is a universally admitted principle of law that what is not forbidden is permitted.

Required or permitted Bible reading suggests more except where plainly forbidden. Eighteen states and the District of Columbia have such laws, and these laws are *prima facie* evidence that Bible teaching is permitted if not suggested. Indeed eleven of the eighteen do not have the restriction "without comment" and thus plainly hold the door wide open for more.

Laws forbidding sectarian instruction. Laws forbidding doctrines on which Christians differ is tacit admission of doctrines on which they agree. And this applies in many states.

No distinction in constitutions between prisons and schools on matters religious. Christianity is freely taught and supported with public funds in prison and thus must be equally right in schools.

No distinction in constitutions between Bible reading and Bible teaching. The first is generally legal, so the last must be.

No distinction in constitutions between Old and New Testaments. Where the first is used the last must be legal.

Christianity formerly universal in schools. Thus it must be legal today, since no recent law forbids it.

Wide use of religion in government, without discrimination against Christianity. Christ in all government except the schools would be a devil's joke, unbelievable to thoughtful people.

Words of supreme courts. No case has reached a supreme court involving more than Bible reading, but several have urged much more—even Bible teaching, and some have mentioned the New Testament.

The Wisconsin Court:

> "There is much in the Bible that is not sectarian. . . . It may be used to inculcate good morals. No better code of morals exists than is contained in the New Testament."—76 Wis. 177.

The Georgia Court mentions "instruction in the Christian religion" in the schools, implying not that the legislature has required it but may do so.

"A Christian may complain as a taxpayer, when
the legislature authorizes such reading of the Bible
or instruction in the Christian religion . . . as gives
one Christian sect preference over others."—152
Ga. 762.

The Colorado Court says some things in the Bible "must be taught."

"Certain studies plainly essential to good citizenship must be taught . . . much in the Bible is essential to good citizenship."—81 Colo. 276.

The Kansas Court wants the lives of noble Bible characters studied in the schools:

"The noblest ideals of moral character are found
in the Bible. To emulate these is the supreme
conception of citizenship. It could not therefore
have been the intention of the framers of the constitution to impose the duty upon the legislature of
establishing a system of common schools where
morals are inculcated and to exclude therefrom
the lives of the persons who possessed the highest
moral attainments."—69 Kan. 53.

The Kentucky Court urged study of the life of Christ and much more:

"The history of religion, including its teachings
and claims of authority . . . might be profitably
studied. Why not also the wisdom of Solomon and
the life of Christ?"—120 Ky. 609.

The Federal Supreme Court held it to be in harmony with Christian principles to teach the New Testament in this land:

> "Why may not the Bible, and especially the New Testament . . . be read and taught . . . expounded . . . explained . . . inculcated?"—2 Howard 200.

The same high Court (262 U. S. 404), standing on the Fourteenth Amendment to the Federal Constitution, decreed:

> "No state shall make or enforce any law that shall abridge the privileges or immunities of citizens of the United States."

Thus it forbade exclusion of the German language from the schools on the ground that such knowledge is "not injurious to health, morals or beyond the understanding of any ordinary child." There is little doubt that if a case were carried to that high Court, just as was the German language case, that body would hold the Christian religion rightfully in the schools.

Teaching morals in school. Schoolmen say, "Character is the highest aim of all education," and our laws generally require moral instruction in public schools. Christian morals are the standard of conduct in this country, and Christianity the soil in which the best morals grow.

185

By no line of reasoning can moral teaching be required as it is, and Christian teaching excluded from the schools of this country.

Present widespread return of Christ to the schools. All this, with no change of law, with no serious trouble from any source, with hearty support of parents, as will appear in a subsequent chapter, is ample proof that not new law but a new psychology is our great need today.

The District of Columbia is not a state but a Federal district ruled by Congress under Federal law. Since 1866, perhaps much longer, by law, religious exercises, not excluding the Master of men, including daily Bible reading, hymn singing, and the Lord's Prayer, have been the daily custom in all schoolrooms of the nation's capital city. This should be good evidence that Christian teaching in the schools is in harmony with the principles of our government, especially when taken with what is said in point two above. The enemy himself being the judge, no question of legality is involved. At least the law has never been attacked in the courts.

The above does not mean that no new law is

needed, for we do need new legislation, not so much to legalize as to provide a definite program and to protect teachers in giving the instruction. But one of the great needs is a new psychology—a definite realization that the religion of this Christian nation has a perfect right and must have the right-of-way in all departments of our educational system.

Note. What is said in these pages about the absence of religion from public education is as true of higher education as of the common schools. It is notorious that the cry for academic freedom so loudly voiced in state universities is often used to tear down but never to build up religious ideals. It is equally true that religion is as rightfully in universities as in common schools, for the law makes no distinction.

Compulsory Study of Religion

What does religious liberty mean? Jefferson, the author of the *Statute of Religious Freedom,* wrote the Danbury Baptist Association: "A man has no natural rights in opposition to his social duties." The Federal Supreme Court quoted and relied upon those words in outlawing polygamy in Utah (98 U. S. 156), and said that under religious liberty "Congress was left free to reach actions which are in violation of social duties and subversive of good order." In 186 U. S. 393, the Supreme Court faced the whole question of personal versus social rights and said:

> "For the public good individuals must suffer destruction of property or even life, rights of necessity being part of the law, and the possession and enjoyment of all rights are subject to such reasonable conditions as may be decreed by the governing authority essential to safety, health, peace, good order and morals of the community."

Without becoming too technical, Bible reading in school may be an act of worship or of obtaining knowledge, as the hearer desires. Study of religion would not be an act of worship but of obtaining knowledge. Not even God can force anyone to worship nor to believe the knowledge obtained. But obtaining knowledge is not a matter of belief; it is an act, a practice. Government requires that practices, in religion or what not, conform to the peace of society. So this writer is firmly convinced that government, as super-parent, may if it wishes, rightfully require a child to listen to Bible reading or engage in study of religion, all of course in the hope that the child will believe the truth learned and live it. But where only an occasional child would decline to study or listen, the government might well wink at the vagary and excuse the child.

A single illustration will show how the matter herein considered may, through misunderstanding, cease to be religious liberty and become tyranny, and, if widely applied, work great harm to the nation. In January, 1925, 30,-000 citizens of Portland, Oregon, a city of 300,-000, petitioned the school board to have daily Bible reading in all schools. The board was favorable until one citizen objected, insisting that the practice would violate the religious liberty of his child in school and demanding that the petition be refused. A member of the board said, "Of course if any citizen objects we have no right to adopt the rule," and the board turned down the petition.

All this objector had a right to do was to ask that his child be excused, and the board could have adopted the Bible-reading rule and then excused the child of the objector.

Content of Christian Teaching

The difficulty today seems to be that teachers fear to put any religion into the schools, to say nothing of Christian truth. The fear is groundless as shown by the fact that the whole Bible may be in the schools, including the truths upon which Christians agree. But what truths do all Christians accept?

Unitarians are conceded to be most to the left of any Christian group, and it might be well to hear what they say. W. E. Channing was probably the greatest preacher that company has produced; and, though he lived a century ago, leaders of that faith seemed less than fifty years ago to consider him still their chief apostle. In 1896, the American Unitarian Association published a large volume of his writings and sent them broadcast to ministers over the nation. He said:

> "The doctrines which Christianity commits to its teachers (preachers) are mighty engines. The perfect character of God; the tender and solemn attributes which belong to Him as our Father and Judge; the character and history of Christ; his intimate union with his followers; his sufferings and cross; his resurrection, ascension and inter-

190

cession; the promised aid of the Holy Spirit; immortality of man."[1]

Again:

"We deny the Christian name to none who acknowledge Jesus as Saviour and Lord. . . . The historical and miraculous proofs of Christianity are indeed essential and impregnable."[2]

Concerning Christian teaching in public schools he says:

"We would not of course admit into schools the peculiarities of denominations that divide the Christian world. The young mind should be guided through nature and human history to the Creator and Disposer of the universe; and, still more, the practical principles of Christianity should be matters of direct inculcation."[3]

Horace Mann and Thomas Jefferson, two of the greatest friends of religious public education that the nation has produced, were both Unitarians, and would doubtless heartily endorse the above words of their leader.

Since the days of these torchbearers, we have gone far from the road they pointed out as the safe way in public education, and it will take us a long time to come back, but come back we must if the nation is to survive.

GOD IN OUR PUBLIC SCHOOLS

REFERENCES

1 *Channing's Works, New Edition Complete.* American Unitarian Association, Boston, 1896, p. 277.
2. Ibid., p. 274.
3. Ibid., p. 123.

XI

CHRISTIAN PUBLIC EDUCATION ESSENTIAL

So far we have considered only the *right* of the state to teach religion and have found no obstacle. Now we face the *duty* of the state in that regard. Chapter VII shows that the child, parents, church, citizens generally, each and all, have certain natural rights touching the subject. Here we hold that under religious liberty the state is in duty bound to see that these rights be granted and guarded. We urge now that CHRISTIAN PUBLIC EDUCATION IS AN ESSENTIAL DUTY OF THE STATE. *We are sure that the state, which assumes the role of super-parent, as it does and must, and compels every child to go to school, must also assume the same role and rule in the study of religion. We are sure, too, that the religion we put into our schools must be the Christian religion, the religion of this nation.*

In the light of previous discussion, perhaps

rather brief consideration only is needed here.

1. The life of the nation is at stake.

Thoughtful people agree with the *New York Sun* of September 10, 1894:

> "The religious force is one of the controlling elements of civilization. A generation that grows up with no greater fear of wrong than the policeman's club will never be a law-abiding nation."

The most shocking tragedy of the present World War was the sudden collapse of France in face of the German war machine. Now comes word over the radio and in news reports from the present rulers of that proud but humble nation that the unspeakable tragedy is the result of the weakening of the moral fibre of the nation's youth growing out of the absence of religion from their public schools and that, in penitence and humility, France is restoring religion to her schools. The tragedy of France warns America of the fate that awaits her if she continues her present policy of shutting the schoolhouse door in the face of God. The verdict of history agrees with the word of Holy Writ that the nation that forgets God will perish. Every believer in God believes that. Only atheists deny it, and to follow them means destruction.

Again we quote from the startling address of C. C. Morrison before the ten thousand teachers of Missouri in Kansas City last fall:

> "Protestant children in public schools are under an influence with which the churches cannot compete and which they cannot counteract. The public school presents the church with a generation of youth whose minds have been cast in a secular mold. . . . You can educate every child in America in the subjects taught in our public schools and yet our democracy may go down . . . . The last stand of democracy will be in the realm of the people's faith. . . . The Christian religion is the inner citadel of democracy. . . . Democracy is Christianity's gift to the world. And when Christianity fails, democracy fails. The only solution as I see it, is to open the public schools to include the teaching of religion."

We have seen religion struggling and relatively declining and crime growing by leaps and bounds for half a century. If we only stop to think, we shall know that the tide must soon turn or the nation will face disaster. We have seen that other suggested remedies cannot avail. We have found that mere Bible reading in the public schools seems to help some, but that it cannot solve the problem. Thoughtful men at the beginning and along the way have warned that only God in the schoolhouse would save us from tragedy. *Beyond question we must again, as in early days, permeate our public educational system with the moral and religious message of the Man of Galilee, or the nation will perish.*

2. **Our fundamental principles must be perpetuated.** For a century and a half we Americans have enjoyed a new experience in the world, the sweets of religious liberty and separation of church and state. We will never give them up without a battle to the death. But only nonsectarian Christian national standards can hope to retain those principles. Now, the crime wave and the struggle of the churches join farseeing men in urging that only nonsectarian Christian teaching in the public schools can hold our necessary national standards. Therefore if we would continue to enjoy the fruits, we must meet the conditions and restore and hold God in public education.

3. **Crooks, racketeers, radicals must be**

eliminated. "A man trained in mind but not in morals is a menace to society," said Theodore Roosevelt. Keen wit and a dull conscience may make "clever devils," to use Huxley's term. We see here what the fathers knew, and we have forgotten that to make safe citizens, religious training is fully as important as mental training. The keener the brain, the more dangerous it is unless steadied by an equivalent religious training. A boy trained in mind but not in morals and religion is mighty good soil for the radicalism now sweeping the nation in these second-world-war days; Naziism, Fascism, Communism, Totalitarianism. From the same soil spring labor racketeers that now bog down industry, delay production, endanger the nation until the army has to be called out to protect men who want to work. From the same soil come crooked politicians and crooked business men and all other dangerous elements of the nation. These are either irreligious or anti-religious. They ply their trade everywhere and all the time and threaten the very life of the nation. Christ in the schoolhouse is the only insurance policy we can get against this breed.

4. **The people must be protected in the enjoyment of their national rights.** We saw in Chapter VII that the child, parent, church, and citizens generally have certain natural rights that only the state can guarantee. Every one of these rights touches the very heart of the nation, and the nation that neglects them does so at her peril. These rights can be safeguarded only by putting the religion of this nation into our schools.

5. **Public education must not be endangered.** Because of its inherent weaknesses, the movement for released-time weekday schools will disappear. The next step will probably be co-operation between the more liberal church groups in organizing Christian parochial schools and withdrawing their children from the public schools, which will take millions of them. The nonreligious public school now makes two suggestions in that direction, both injurious to itself. (a) It penalizes its present loyal patrons who would gladly have religion in the schools. (b) It puts a premium upon the parochial school. The public school with no God in it is a plain invitation to religious par-

198

ents to set up parochial schools. Such a movement would greatly weaken our public school system, the very heart of democracy, and of course do much to destroy the solidarity and therefore the strength of democracy. *The only safety for our public school system is Christ in the schoolhouse.*

6. **Christian morals must be taught.** The very life of the nation depends upon it. Every believer in religion of any kind holds that good morals grow only in a religious soil. "Good character is the highest aim of all education," say educators. The law of nearly all the states now require public schools to teach morals, but such teaching is not there, for with the Bible gone, teachers know they cannot teach right conduct. Judge Lewis L. Fawcett, of the Supreme Court of New York, said: "More than 4,000 of the 8,000 prisoners sentenced by me in thirty years on the bench, were under twenty-one years, and only three were members of Sunday schools at the time of committing the crime." Christian morals are the noblest the race has found, and only such offered to every child at school can save America.

A False Assumption

It is often assumed by some good people that the church is the final authority and guardian of religion. The assumption is wholly without foundation in logic or law. *The Bible is just as much the state's book as it is the church's book. No law of God or man gives the church any pre-eminence over the the state in the right and duty to use and promote religion.* So long as a religious citizenship is necessary to the life of the state, the natural right of self-defense gives the state a perfect right to foster religion—indeed it gives the state a duty to that end.

7. **The Biblical foundations of democracy must be maintained. The Bible is our source of democracy.** In that old college textbook, *The State,* Prof. Woodrow Wilson tells us, "The political institutions of the United States are all in their main features simply the political institutions of England." Even in those old college days we wondered a bit. Whence our written Constitution, our elective ruler, our absence of caste, our universal manhood suffrage, our universal equality which are

the very roots of democracy? These are some things Professor Wilson did not explain.

In his illuminating little book, *The Divine Right of Democracy,* Clarence True Wilson has a chapter on "The Forgotten Sources of Our Federal Constitution." He might have called it "The Divine Source of Democracy." He insists that practically all the undergirding principles of our democracy came from the Bible. He says that "the two most colossal blunders of government" are "a royal family" and "the law of primogeniture." He holds that "the American idea of selecting rulers by merit and not by birthright is from the Scriptures." He thinks that only the Bible shows that rulers should be chosen by merit, and that in this respect our government is the exact reverse of all governments up to our time. He notes eighteen parallels between our governmental principles and those of the old Israelitish commonwealth, and some of them are really surprising. He closes the chapter with these suggestive words:

> "These facts and parallels remind us afresh that our fathers were the first group of Bible-reading men who ever sat down to devise a form of govern-

ment, and it is easy when you consider the history of the Pilgrim Fathers and the religious antecedents of the other settlers of the New World to understand the part the Bible must have played in the development and in the guiding of the fathers in avoidance of the two colossal blunders of all the nations, enabling them to steer safely between these rocks into the haven of democracy."[1]

The above author is not the only man who has noted these facts. Oscar Straus, a Jewish member of the Cabinet of Theodore Roosevelt, called attention to them, as has also Judge M. R. Morris, an eminent jurist and university law professor. Whether these men are wholly right or not, one thing is true, the root idea of democracy, the brotherhood of man, came from that lowly Nazarene who taught the world to say, *"Our Father."* We believe that only as He continues an effective force in America will democracy survive.

Testimony of Our Presidents

The testimony of those just quoted are supported by that of many of America's greatest statesmen. The testimony of a few of these follow:

Thomas Jefferson: "The Bible is the corner-stone of liberty."

Andrew Jackson: "The Bible is the rock on which our republic rests."

Ulysses S. Grant: "To this Book we are indebted for the progress made in our civilization, and to this Book we must look as our guide in the future."

William McKinley: "The more profoundly we study this wonderful Book and the more closely we observe its divine precepts, the better citizens we will become and the higher will be the destiny of our nation."

Herbert Hoover: "We are indebted to the Book of books for our ideals and institutions. Their preservation rests in adhering to its principles."

The all-important question is, If our democracy or any considerable part of it comes from the Bible, just how are we to retain it and discard the Bible? *No question but that if we keep the Bible out of our schools we will discard it from American life.* With his usual brevity,

President Coolidge said, "We cannot reject the cause and retain the results." Horace Mann declared that if religion leaves the schools, democracy is doomed through "profligacy, licentiousness, and corrupt civilization." There are multitudes of Americans who believe that our democracy is in danger today, not only from external foes, but also from radicalism within our own ranks that flouts every principle of our government that stands in its way. And it is not our democracy only. Our democracy seems to be the last battleground of civilization, and if it fails, civilization will be headed for the jungle. We are quite sure that with the proper training of our youth for citizenship, we Americans can take the lead in the solution of international problems. AS GOES AMERICA AT THIS FATEFUL TIME, SO GOES THE WORLD. In short, it is Christ in American schools or chaos for civilization.

God's Message to America

Moses, lawgiver and prophet of God. Excepting the Man of Galilee, no greater man ever trod this globe than that old Bible hero, Moses. The world has known no expert to equal him in the matters now before us. Probably no words in history are so important to America at this time as the words of the aged departing Moses to his own people of long ago. They are found in the first six chapters of the book of Deuteronomy. At first he tells them how marvelously God has led and cared for them for forty years. Then he turns to their future. In the fifth chapter he repeats the Ten Commandments. In the fourth and sixth chapters he pleads with them like a father to be true to God and His law. No fewer than twenty-four times he urges them to love God, obey God, keep the law of God, be faithful to God, walk in the ways of God. He assures them that if they obey and love God, the nation will prosper and become great. He warns that if they forget God, the nation will perish. Several times he urges them to teach the law of God to their children with all the diligence at their command.

The world knows the sequel. As long as Israel obeyed God and taught His law to her children, the nation flourished. When Israel forgot God and turned to idols, the nation was divided and the greater part lost to history— one of the unsolved tragedies of the ages. The smaller part, sometimes faithful, sometimes false, yet more false than faithful, at last lost national existence, and now for almost 2,000 years has wandered over the earth, a nation without a country, a people without a flag, the most persecuted race in the annals of history. In Christian lands only do they have an asylum where they may lay their heads in peace—a peace that will abide only while Christ is in the schools.

In short, if America would live and flourish, she must obey God and teach her children to obey God, teach them in the schools of the land, the only place the nation can teach them. That is the message of our great men, the message of Moses, the message of God to America today.

For encouragement and direction, it may be well to see what is being done in the schools today.

REFERENCE

1. Wilson, C. T., *The Divine Right of Democracy*, p. 29.

XII

THE TEACHER AND THE PROGRAM

A religious teacher is essential to a religious program, and if we have the last we must have the first.

The Teacher

In the old days with religion in all schools, teachers were religious. An elderly Quaker, dean of an Iowa State Teachers College, said to me, "Nearly all teachers are religious. There seems to be something about teaching that attracts religious people." Pastors at times have complained that out-of-town teachers show themselves not religious by absence from church when in town over week ends, and teachers have replied that under existing conditions they hesitate to show their colors. As God returns to the schools, the few nonreligious teachers will seek other employment or be weeded out by school authorities. Some school boards require a promise from out-of-town applicants that they will attend church if in town over Sunday. School boards often ask applicants of what church, if any, they are members and quietly drop the unchurched applicant. The religious attitude and complexion of one school board was quietly changed at the spring election, and by that means an anti-religious school head lost his job, and the Bible was restored to the schools of that city of over 100,000 people. Several states by law, forbid school officials to raise the religious question. Such a law is of doubtful constitutionality, is pagan, and will paganize the schools of that state.

Rights of teachers. It is contended that laws requiring religion in the schools would deny teachers their rights by tending to eliminate those who are not religious. No teacher has a right that runs counter to the common good. Schools are not made for teachers, but to make a safe and enduring nation. When Thomas Jefferson and James Madison, authors of religious liberty, found Professor Thomas Cooper not satisfactory as a teacher in the University of Virginia because of his religious views,

though completely acceptable in everything
else, they quietly dismissed him (Chapter VI),
thus interpreting the principle they put into
American law. When months ago that New
York mother showed the court that the teachings of Bertrand Russell would injure the
morals of her grown daughter student, the court
quickly set aside the contract between Russell
and the school. Hence, unsatisfactory teachers
have a perfect right to hunt another job.

Leading teachers know the job. The best book
ever written on religious education came from
the National Educational Association in 1915.
It is entitled, *The Essential Place of Religion
in Education*. It contained an outline for
religious-moral training from the first grade
through high school. Teachers are religious.
They are broad-minded. They are patriotic.
They are awake to the moral and religious needs
of the time. They know educational methods.
They know child psychology. They know the
schools are not delivering the goods. If we give
them a free hand and support them at the task,
we have nothing to fear from the teachers.

Teacher training in religion. When Horace

Mann set up normal schools in Massachusetts, he required all students to study *The Principles of Piety and Morality Common to All Sects of Christians,* and the Bible was read daily to all students. Our rather limited investigation shows that in some sections we have departed from the pattern he set. Recently, answering our letters, an Illinois State Teachers College said: "The college offers no courses in religion and ethics at any time. This is a state teachers' institution." A similar Indiana school gave like information. The Iowa State Teachers College at Cedar Falls has a good elective course in Bible. So also has the State Teachers College of Kalamazoo, Michigan. Western Maryland (church) College at Westminster magnifies the religious note and co-operates well with state authorities in placing teachers. The best we have seen is a church school, Geneva College, Beaver Falls, in Western Pennsylvania, where in 1941, among a hundred graduates, thirty were given the degree of Bachelor of Science in Education, after very thorough required training in Bible. Thus, young people can today get proper training to teach religion and have reasonable assurance of a fruitful field in that line. Of textbooks to help in schoolroom work below high school, we are very sorry to say that in religion and morals, the field seems wholly barren today; therefore teachers must pioneer.

The Program

No one can say just what should be the content of the religious program for the schools. But we can trust our teachers a long way. If we tell them we want definite religious and Christian ethical instruction as an essential element in all schools and grades, and protect them in giving it, they will work out the details of a satisfactory program. Following are some items now found in different schools that might well be in all. These are not given here so much for teachers as to show the public what can be done.

Daily religious worship. Formerly this was universal. Many teachers now observe the custom from personal wish. Forty million people in twelve states and many great cities and villages, by requirement of law, now have such services in their schools. This is largely a recent return to a former practice. Some of this is doubtless perfunctory, halfhearted, performed as duty, hurried through to get at things considered more important. Teachers who feel that way about it should seek other employment, since the teacher is the key to the situation. These moments are highly important, essential to right training and right living for every child. During this time the schoolroom should be the nation's family altar, where teacher and children all bow in love and reverence before the common Father of us all in a few minutes of worship at the beginning of the day. Religious songs should be sung. Prayer should be offered by the teacher or the Lord's Prayer repeated in unison. A passage of religious or moral value should be read from the Bible—not from a book of Bible selections. Simple explanation or clarifying comments should be permitted, though carefully used. There should be nothing sectarian. For small children a few passages often repeated would be best. A child should be excused on request, but no such suggestion should come from the teacher. The absence, if requested and granted, will probably not be long continued. Such service for ten minutes would enthrone God in the schoolroom for the entire day, do much to turn America back to God and right living, and open the schoolroom doors to much more teaching of religion and morals.

Bible stories. I sat for two hours one day on the side line, or as that aging Presbyterian pastor, Rev. C. P. Andrews, called it, "the observation car," while he told Bible stories to several hundred children in a public school building within sight of the Michigan state capitol building. First he had about twenty-five kindergartners; then the first and second grades; then the third and fourth; then the fifth and sixth; finally the seventh and eight. Each story took from twenty to twenty-five minutes. The story for the previous week was always reviewed first, the children retelling the story. The advance story was given. Not a thing was over the heads of the children; no effort at effect; no preaching; no moralizing. If God or a moral appeared, they were noted, but not dragged in—merely a Bible story, sweetly and winsomely told. Some stories were from the Old Testament, some from the New Testament. Some were continued, some were not. Each

213

story fitted the group to which it was told. It was a marvelous piece of work. I have never seen more interested children. There was no need for discipline. Teachers stood or sat on the side lines with nothing to do.

This man was telling Bible stories three or four afternoons a week to 1,500 children in half a dozen schoolhouses in several different villages. Teachers, school boards, and parents co-operated beautifully, and no one objected. He had been doing this work for over six years when I heard him. He did it for several years more until age and health called a halt. A recent letter from him notes that he received high commendation from county superintendents of schools in two counties, that parents of 3,000 children in that section of the state now anxiously look for some pastor to take his place. He said that parents of all faiths and of no faith were glad for his work and wanted it continued. One Roman Catholic teacher, going to another section, tried to find a pastor to take up the work. Failing in this she undertook and carried it on herself.

Four other pastors, three Methodists and one Baptist, inspired by his work, took up the task and carried it on in more than a score of village and country schoolhouses. The work continued for some years. But pastors moved, and the work was dropped.

Sitting on the side lines that day, I did some thinking. Thank God for busy pastors who see the need and try to meet it. But why must preachers do the work? Why not schoolteachers? Why do not other teachers follow the lead of that Catholic girl? I saw those teachers sitting on the side lines with folded hands, drinking in the sweetness of the message. But why are their lips sealed? If it is wrong for schoolteachers to tell Bible stories to children in schoolhouses on school time, why is it right for ministers to do it? If it is right for ministers to do it, why is it wrong for regular schoolteachers? We Americans need just a little horse sense. A woman schoolteacher can do a better job of storytelling to children than almost any preacher, even if they are Bible stories. Not a few teachers are doing it today. Why not give every grade teacher in the land a chance at it with the assurance of the school board that she will be supported in the task? If that were started tomorrow in every schoolroom, the paganism now in our educational system would soon begin to disappear like mist before the morning sun, and God would be enthroned in our schools to the immeasurable good of the nation.

Religious instruction in the grades. In Pine Bluff, Arkansas, a city of over 20,000, the school superintendent asked churches to select such religious teachers as they wished. Then he asked all parents to choose which teacher they wanted for their child and sent each child to the teacher requested—all work to be done in schoolhouses on school time. Ten years ago I witnessed this honest but cumbersome effort to do a very important work. It helped educate children in religion, but it tended to promote sectarianism and to use public money for sectarian purposes—the very thing we seek to get away from in religious education.

A bit earlier, we talked with Professor E. H. Drake, superintendent of schools of Kalamazoo, Michigan, a city of 60,000. A specially trained woman, paid at first by the churches, but later from public funds, taught religion to all children from the third to the sixth grades in a public schoolroom on school time. Only one parent ever asked that his child be excused, and after talking with the superintendent, the man told his boy to take the religious training. At my request Professor Drake was invited to give an address on Religious Public Education at a Conference of the National Reform Association. He told of the work mentioned above and of much more being done in the schools of his city—daily Bible reading in all schools, high school chapel exercises, elective Bible study, Bible memory work, religious pageantry, religious dramatization, etc. Professor Drake is now deceased, but his successor in a recent letter says the work still continues as formerly.

The plan used in Kalamazoo for teaching religion is in perfect harmony with every principle of American law and is a great step in the right direction. It is better and simpler than the Pine Bluff plan, and there is no reason why it could not be adopted in schools all over the land. In small places and in rural schools, the individual teacher might have to do all the work.

Religious and moral instruction classes. It is pedagogical fallacy that religion and morals must be caught, not taught, and that the silent influence of the teacher is the best instruction. We suspect such remarks are often excuses for failure to try. Religion and morals can be better caught if taught, and if the words of the teacher support her life. But we know of nothing in print to put into the hands of the teacher to help meet this need, and no doubt this lack explains why so little is being done in our schools. However, a bill covering this very matter now lies on our desk. Whether this bill recently received from Rhode Island ever becomes a law or not, it points to a better day.

Religion and morals in school readers. I examined nine sets of school readers put out by different publishing houses for today's use in the fifth to the eighth grades of our schools. There were thirty different books. They were filled with fables, folk lore, fairy tales, pagan mythology, jingles, and jangles, but not with the religious and moral message of the Book that made our civilization. Two-thirds had no Bible passage, and morals were a minus quantity. About one-half of one per cent was from the Bible, and some of that was not accredited.

There was more of the pagan gods of Greece in one volume than of the God that made the universe in all the thirty. My heart sank as I saw the paganism now being fed to our children in school readers. I got out that old *Mc-Guffey's Fifth Reader,* used very widely in American schools, fifty to a hundred years ago, and almost hugged it. A fourth of its lessons are distinctly religious. In it there is nothing sectarian, but it has many lessons of moral value. Before me lies another reader, used in the sixth grade of a Catholic school. Of two hundred and fourteen pages, eighty-one have a distinct religious flavor. Catholic sectarianism? Yes, some of it, but not a pagan line. I would much sooner have it in the hands of my child than any of the thirty books mentioned above. No wonder priests yearn to get their children out of the public schools. No wonder that Catholic paper, *Our Sunday Visitor*, of September 1, 1940, had a big picture on the front page, "The Empty Throne" of God in public schools. No wonder it began a powerful, almost pathetic plea for the restoration of non-sectarian religion to our public schools, in these words: "To restore God to His place of honor

219

in all the classrooms of the land constitutes the greatest need in American life today." No wonder Archbishop Ireland in 1890 told the teachers of the nation that through secular education "The very life of our civilization is at stake." Why not put that old McGuffey system of readers back into the schools, or even that Catholic reader, and burn the pagan poison being fed to our children today in school readers? Yes, why not even use the Bible as a school reader as was done widely in former days?

High school chapel services. Twenty years ago such a thing was unheard of. When we began our travels, an occasional request came in for an address to high school students, "a talk on morals but not on religion." One superintendent in an Illinois town with, as he said, "five girls gone wrong recently in our high school," requested me, "Mister, give them all you have, the hotter the better." In this line things are improving rapidly. Not long ago a questionnaire was sent to two hundred and one school superintendents in Michigan towns of over 1,000, and one hundred and forty replies were received. The Bible was read daily in all or many schoolrooms of eighty-five towns. Chapel exercises were reported in fifty-eight high schools. Most of these were religious services. A few were merely assemblies. A local pastor was often, if not usually, invited for the occasion, and he came gladly. He was given a Bible and told to read it and pray with the boys and girls and say what he wished. Some of the talks were moral only. Most of them, however, were religious. No student asked to be excused. One pastor overstepped. He gave a sectarian harangue and was not invited back. Priests usually took their turn and were very fine.

No student asked to be excused, and all gave respectful attention. In Lansing, Michigan, the state capital, weekly chapel exercises were held during Lent and a local pastor was asked to preach a sermon. Ordinarily pastors faced eager audiences of 1,000 students and their teachers. Chapel exercises are now quite common in high schools.

High school Bible study classes. Quite a number of those Michigan superintendents replied that they did have a Bible school study class, and that they met in the schoolhouse on schooltime. Some teachers were pastors, some regular schoolteachers. Such courses are now by no means uncommon, though unheard of a few years ago. Schoolteachers took the lead. Early steps were hesitant, but courage came with experience. About 1918, the Iowa State Teachers Association appointed a Quaker, a Catholic, and a Unitarian—all teachers—to prepare a textbook for such study. The resulting book could not but be approved by a Methodist, a Baptist, or a Presbyterian. In 1921, Michigan teachers appointed a committee and the resulting text was very commendable, though its touch upon religion and morals was a bit light and its expectation of being used out of school hours not bold enough. The book prepared by a church college Bible teacher at the behest of the Indiana State Teachers Association was approved and adopted by the Association in 1926, and is of a very high order.[1] All three of these books have gone beyond state lines. The tendency now is to offer elective courses on schooltime, in school buildings, taught by regular schoolteachers.

The best work we have observed was done in Highland Park, Michigan, a city of 80,000, completely surrounded by Detroit. Here Professor S. A. Graves, a regular schoolteacher, conducted such a class for eight or ten years until he became dean of the Detroit Y. M. C. A. College and had to give up the class. He said he had over one hundred students a year and that in six years five hundred high school graduates had taken his course. The Bible study was a regular part of the English course for which full credit was given. He prepared his own outlines. All local religious denominations were usually represented in the class. Religion and morals were openly and freely discussed by teachers and students. The discussion was often controversial but always friendly. He said, "Even if I wanted to give sectarian matters, it would be impossible to get away with it with so many denominations represented." In all the years there was never any trouble in class nor in the community concerning it. When Professor Graves left the school, the class was dropped because no suitable teacher was available.

A county superintendent of schools in Indiana wrote some years ago that the schools employed a trained man who traveled from high school to high school and gave his whole time to Bible teaching.

The Rhode Island bill mentioned above magnifies the moral side of religion and would make the study compulsory all the way through high school, with full credit.

The Bible in foreign language classes. Probably every high school student in America today, when he begins the study of Latin, German, French, Greek, or any other foreign language has for the first two years Caesar's *Gallic Wars,* Baron Munchausen Stories, Xenophon's *Anabasis,* or the like for sample sentences and translation, all valueless today as history, useless as stories, having nothing of moral or religious uplift, good only for the mere words. Would it not be far better to use the Latin Vulgate, Luther's matchless German Bible, the Greek New Testament, a French translation of the Book of books, etc.—deathless history, marvelous stories, noble language, the best of morals and religion, thus building a life while growing in knowledge?

Religious education in rural schools. Just recently we found in the Finger Lake region of New York State a group of Baptist churches with a missionary organization they called The Larger Parish. This organization employs a trained woman who visits many rural schools once a week, during the entire school year, giving school children definite religious instruction in the schoolhouse, on school time, to the great delight of the parents. The effort is most commendable, but it would be far more likely to be permanent, much less open to just criticism on sectarian grounds, quite as satisfactory generally, the expense more evenly distributed, and perfectly legal, if public school authorities did it themselves and paid the bills, employing perhaps the same woman.

God in special subjects. When history is written today, it is meaningless change, no philosophy. If a great battle is won or lost, it was a rainstorm or Blucher or Napoleonic strategy, not God deciding the destiny of nations. If geology or biology be the subject, it is natural evolution. If astronomy, the universe is a self-acting machine. And so on, and on. Why shall evolution be taught as hinting atheism when Darwin said otherwise? When Kant, the greatest of moral philosophers, saw God "in starry heavens above and the moral law within," when Spencer and Haeckel and Einstein find something they cannot fathom, why shall pygmy philosophers prate of the universe as a self-acting machine and drive students to atheism? When college professors become so wise that they know all about everything but God and boast that they are agnostics, it might be well to promote them to the position of professor emeritus. Perhaps it would be well to require that the first verse of the Bible, "In the beginning God," be printed on the title page of all textbooks on natural science. We cannot bring God back to America by admitting atheistic textbooks or agnostic teachers to our schools.

REFERENCE

1. Huffman, J. A., D.D., *A Guide to the Study of the Old and New Testament*, Standard Press, Marion, Indiana. Price, $1.00.

XIII

WHAT NEXT?

What shall churchmen do? Every religious
group in America suffers—Protestant, Catholic, Jew. All have numberless children in the
public schools, getting no religion, growing
up with no knowledge of God and His rules
of conduct—practically pagans, potentially
dangerous citizens, candidates for the prison
cell, without hope in time or eternity. And the
nation suffers. Crime is rampant. No home is
exempt. Our property and lives are in danger.
Our mothers, wives, and daughters may suffer
and die at the hands of rapists.

To those who are in doubt, or have fears about
restoring the Bible and nonsectarian religion
to the public schools, we recommend the words
of Dr. Charles M. Sheldon, author of *In His
Steps* and for many years editor of *The Christian Herald:*

"The danger of using the Bible in our public
schools is nothing as compared to the danger

from not using it." While shepherds remain
apart or fuss over trifles, the wolf slyly drives
off the lambs. How much more sensible to get
together and settle our little differences or
forget them and unitedly go forward to restore
God to his throne in every schoolroom in the
land.

Voluntary Co-operation

Probably the first thing is for the clergy to
learn that the three groups are not and must not
be aliens to each other, but friends and co-oper-
ators in the common and noble task of helping
children to find a right way of life. Next they
must learn that church and school are not two
separate worlds with an impassable gulf between and that churchmen and schoolmen do
not belong to antagonistic races.

It is also highly important to know that
Protestants, Catholics, and Jews believe every
word found in the various versions of the Old
Testament used by Protestants, except that
Jews do not accept two brief words in Isaiah
about the wonderful name and the virgin birth.

Furthermore the recent Catholic translation
of the New Testament should be acceptable to

Protestants as well as Catholics and much of it would be satisfactory to Jews. Thus in the Catholic version of the New Testament and the Protestant versions of the Old Testament we have a common ground of truth acceptable to Catholics and Protestants. A Jewish child also could accept all the Old Testament, except as above, and much of the New Testament. It should be known, too, that at the World's Parliament of Religions in Chicago in 1893, devotees of every known religon, day after day, joined in the Lord's Prayer. Thus we have here so nearly a common ground of religious faith and practice that it would be of inestimable value as a basis of religion for use in all public schools.

Probably in many communities the move to return the Bible to the school will start with the Protestant ministers. After agreement among themselves, they should contact the priest and then the rabbi if such there be in the community. Experience has shown that these men are approachable on the subject, and that a large part of our trouble has been that leaders have remained apart or have argued together and prayed apart. In such friendly conference, it would seem that daily Bible reading and the Lord's Prayer could become with unanimous approval the daily practice in all schools—no child required to join but all permitted to do so. Then it should be easy to conceive a Bible story hour for all children with a state-paid teacher, chosen from the school staff, acceptable to all parties. Why not also have a weekly chapel service in high school with priest, pastor, and rabbi invited to give religious talks and lead in prayer?

Then let a meeting be called of the clergy, of all groups—of the parent-teachers' association, of the officers and teachers of the school and others interested—and the above program presented, discussed, and, if possible, adopted. Such effort and result is in perfect harmony with every principle of our government. It would seem feasible in almost every community, and it would put church and school in helpful co-operation, as they should be. This is only a start. Much more could be done. Of course if any religious group declines to co-operate, the rest must go on.

Protection to teachers. Teachers should not

be expected to go ahead on their own initiative, for that would lay them open to attack by some opponent. *School boards and legislatures should adopt mandatory measures, not to compel teachers but to take responsibility off their shoulders and put it upon the people— where it belongs.*

Bible Reading Law

As noted above much can be done in many sections by local people to restore God to the schools, but in many places nothing will be done, and only a state law will meet the need. The first law to be enacted should be what is now the law in twelve states, a law that requires the daily reading of a portion of the Bible in every schoolroom. The present Maine law is probably the best we have upon the subject. The governor of that state did a wise thing when he asked the state superintendent of schools to prepare a bill and seek its passage. The bill became law and is given here in full as a suggestion:

"To secure greater security in the faith of our fathers, to inculcate into the lives of the rising generation the spiritual values necessary to the well-being of our future civilization, to develop

231

those high moral and religious principles necessary to human happiness, to make available to the
youth of the land the Book which has been the
inspiration of the greatest masterpieces of literature, art, and music, and which has been the
strength of the great men and women of the Christian era, there shall be in the public schools of the
state, daily or at suitable intervals, readings from
the Scriptures with special emphasis upon the Ten
Commandments, the Psalms of David, Proverbs
of Solomon, the Sermon on the Mount, and the
Lord's Prayer. It is provided further that there
shall be no denominational or sectarian comment
or teaching, and each pupil shall give respectful
attention, but shall be free in his own forms of worship."

What shall schoolmen do? There is a widespread call for a group of clergymen—Protestant, Catholic, Jewish—to prepare an outline
of materials suitable for religious public education. The purpose is good, but the plan is
basically wrong. The logical suggestion from
it would be that only those fitted to prepare the
program are fitted to teach the subject—the
mistake widely made today when religion is
returning to the schools. It would also belittle
schoolteachers, tend to leave religion out of
their preparatory training, to disregard the

character of teachers, and to keep religion out of other subjects where it has a vital place. A better and a perfectly satisfactory way would be along the lines of the bill recently introduced into the Rhode Island legislature. The bill failed to pass, not because it was bad but probably because it was new and therefore not well considered. It said:

> "The Director of Education shall make a study of the curricula offered by the public schools within this state for the purpose of prescribing a course of study to be known as a course in morals and religion, in which there shall be classes in Bible study with special emphasis on analysis of the Ten Commandments, the training of pupils to have no sectarian or denominational character of any kind and the emphasis to be placed upon moral values and teachings."

The comment here is not upon the program, but upon the method of preparing it. A state officer is to supervise the work, which is proper. As to details, that officer may use whom he pleases, and it would be proper for him to appoint a mixed group, clergy and teachers, all three faiths represented in proper proportion. Probably the relation of the clergy should be that of a consultative nature on the religious program only, leaving details of carrying it out to the regular educational part of the group.

Bible Teaching Law

A bill prepared in line with the thought above might well contain provisions as noted below—title, enacting clause, responsibility, constitutionality, etc., being added by the legislature.

THE PREAMBLE

WHEREAS, In the interest of the public welfare, the state is the ultimate guardian of every child; and

WHEREAS, In the language of the Ordinance for the government of the Northwest Territory, "Religion, morality, and knowledge are necessary to good government and the happiness of mankind," and

WHEREAS, In the words of Washington, "Reason and experience both forbid us to expect that national morality can prevail in exclusion of religious principles," and

WHEREAS, According to Webster's dictum, "The right of the state to punish crime, involves its duty to teach morality"; and

WHAT NEXT?

WHEREAS, The religious and moral standards of this state and nation are those of the Bible,

Section 1. Immediately upon the passage of this act, the state department of public instruction shall prepare courses in nonsectarian religion and morals suitable for all grades of the common and high schools of this state, with special emphasis upon the Ten Commandments, the Shepherd Psalm, the Proverbs, the Sermon on the Mount, the Lord's Prayer, the Golden Rule, and the Judicial Oath used in all our courts. High schools shall also include courses in the historical and literary value of the Bible.

Section 2. Prior to the opening of school in the fall of . . . and regularly thereafter, the state department of public instruction shall ascertain from all public school teachers and applicants as special teachers of said courses their willingness, fitness, and ability to teach said courses, and shall grant certificates to all who meet the required tests, and teachers of said courses shall be chosen from holders of such certificates. No sectarian test shall be applied, and teachers not holding such certificates shall not be discriminated against as teachers of other subjects.

Section 3. At the beginning of the fall term of school in . . . . said courses shall become and thereafter shall be required in all grades of the common and high schools of this state and shall be taught not less than one hour each week.

Section 4.   Beginning in the fall of . . . all state teachers' colleges in this state shall require all students entering at that time and thereafter to take a one-year course in religion and morals prepared in harmony with the provisions hereof, and on and after said date said colleges shall offer elective courses in the historical and literary values of the Bible.

Section 5.   Nothing herein shall be interpreted as forbidding other nonsectarian religious or moral instruction in addition to what is here specified for use in the schools.

Another highly desirable law would require those charged with the purchase of readers and supplementary readers for the common schools to look with special favor upon such as contain Bible selections of religious and moral worth.

Helpful Agencies

Gideons. For many years these Christian business men, traveling salesmen, not ministers, have been placing Bibles in hotel rooms throughout America. Recently they have enlarged the field of their work to include the placing of Bibles in our public schools. Their goal is a Bible on every teacher's desk in America. They raise the money to provide these Bibles. Already they have presented, with dedicatory exercises, to public school authorities as many as 171,880 Bibles, and this work has only begun. Their voice is a powerful appeal to men of business for the return of God to public education.

Women's clubs. On May 21, 1941, in Atlantic City, Mrs. John L. Whitehurst, incoming president of the General Federation of Women's Clubs, gave an address, "The Return of Religion." She held truly that this country is built upon a "religious foundation," and urged the return of religion to public schools. Now the Home Department of that great body announces as one of its four aims "to urge the school authorities to teach the fundamentals of the religious life." Thus this great body of women, one of the most powerful in the nation, will carry a strong appeal to every corner of the land to re-enthrone God in all schools.

The Woman's Christian Temperance Union. For many years this organization has been very active for the return of God to the public schools, and it has a special department devoted to that effort. The author is well acquainted with the national president, Mrs. Ida B. Wise Smith, and remembers her interest in and work for this cause in Iowa. It was the Arkansas state organization of this body that started and joined in the movement that restored the Bible to the schools of Arkansas in 1930. They have done pioneer and most creditable work in many states for many years on behalf of the Bible in the schools, and their efforts have reached down into local communities in all parts of the land.

Thus the women of America will help tremendously to turn us from secularism and crime to safety and progress.

Parent-Teacher Associations. These thousands of groups meeting in schoolhouses, can, if they will, make a most compelling appeal. Here parents can speak out for their own children. Here thoughtful parents can plead for the children of thoughtless and incompetent parents—those underprivileged children in every community. Here ministers and church leaders may speak out and urge that public schools no longer cast their influence, unintentionally but actually, against the churches and religion. Here the appeal can be made in close and friendly contact with school board and teachers. Here is the court of last resort except the ballot.

Individuals in strategic positions. Governors of states, superintendents of public instruction, judges in boys' courts, Christian men in legislatures, ministers in the pulpit, editors in their papers, private citizens exercising the right of petition, voters at the ballot box, all have a right and must speak out, urging that we put God back into the public schools, and thus bring America back to moral and religious safety.

THE END

INDEX

INDEX

to safeguard public schools,
198

to maintain Biblical foundations of democracy, 200

why legal, 181-186

Churches not at fault, 67

Church statisticians' difficulties, 63, 64

Cincinnati case, 48, 49

Claxton, P. P., ex-Commissioner of Education of U. S., 137

Compulsory study of religion, 187, 189

Conflict in the field of morality, 89

Coolidge, Calvin, 33, 56, 204

Cooper, Thomas, 118

Co-operation between Protestants, Catholics, and Jews, 15, 228, 230

Crafts, Wilbur R., 62

Crime,

growth of, 57-61

American Bar Association on, 57

in states with required Bible reading compared with states where not required, 71-73

p r i m a r y and secondary causes of, 67-69

D

Declaration of Independence, faith in God underlies, 10

Democracy, divine source of, 201

rooted in religious faith, 9

Dewey, John, 129

District of Columbia, daily Bible reading and religious exercises in schools, 186

Drake, Prof. E. H., 216

Dunn, Judge, 59

E

Eighteenth Amendment, 24

F

Fawcett, Judge Lewis F., 199

Federal Bureau of Investigation Chart, facing, 59

Finley, John H., 32, 54

Fleming, W. S.,

personal experience, 66

Dr. Weigle's estimate of his book, 12

France, tragedy of, 194

Fundamental principles, 94-122

G

Gabriel, Prof. Ralph, 9

General Federation Women's Clubs include Bible teaching in schools in their aims, 237

Germany, schools of, 23, 24

Gideons supply B i b l e s to schools, 226

Girard Will Case, 171

God's Message to America, 204

in special subjects, 225

Grant, U. S., 203

Graves, Prof. S. A., 223

INDEX

INDEX

INDEX

INDEX

with decisions on Bible in public schools, 145, 156

T

Tax money,
forbidden for sectarian purposes, 46, 51
sectarian use of, 49
Teachers,
generally religious, 207
know their job, 209
rights of, 208
Teacher training and religion, 209
Teaching morals in public schools, 185
Trinity Court Case, "This is a Christian nation," 111

U

Unchurched children and youth, 66
United States, a Christian nation, 111
United States Supreme Court on Bible and religion in schools, 156, 170, 185, 188
University of Illinois, 42
University of Michigan, 41

University of Virginia, 40, 116-120
important place of religion in, 119

V

Virginia,
a Christian state, 103, 104
struggle over religious liberty, 97, 106
Vitamin in public school religion, 13

W

Washington, George, 43, 61
Webster, Daniel, 134
Webster, Noah, 37
Weigle, Luther A., 9-12, 27, 52, 54, 85, 89
Wheedon, D. D., 42
Whitehurst, Mrs. John L., 238
Williams, Roger, 95
Wilson, Clarence True, 201
Wilson, Woodrow, 200
"Without note or comment," 46, 47, 179
Woman's Christian Temperance Union, 237
Women's Clubs, Federation of, 237